Antonio García Cubas, George F. Henderson

The Republic of Mexico in 1876

A political and ethnographical Division of the Population, Character, etc.

Antonio García Cubas, George F. Henderson

The Republic of Mexico in 1876

A political and ethnographical Division of the Population, Character, etc.

ISBN/EAN: 9783337134099

Printed in Europe, USA, Canada, Australia, Japan

Cover: Foto ©ninafisch / pixelio.de

More available books at **www.hansebooks.com**

THE
REPUBLIC OF MEXICO
IN 1876.

A POLITICAL AND ETHNOGRAPHICAL DIVISION OF THE POPULATION,
CHARACTER,
HABITS, COSTUMES AND VOCATIONS OF ITS INHABITANTS

WRITTEN IN SPANISH
BY
ANTONIO GARCIA CUBAS
Author of various geographical
and statistical treatises respecting the same Republic

TRANSLATED INTO ENGLISH
BY
GEORGE F. HENDERSON.

*Illustrated with plates of the principal types of the ethnographic families
and several specimens of popular music*

MEXICO
"LA ENSEÑANZA" PRINTING OFFICE
PORTAL DE MERCADERES N. 7
—
1876

TO

WILLIAM BARRON ESQUIRE

AS A TESTIMONIAL OF ESTEEM AND GRATITUDE

HIS OBEDIENT SERVANT

ANTONIO GARCIA CUBAS.

This book has been written with the view of removing the wrong impressions that may have been left on the minds of the readers of those works which, with evil intent or with the desire of acquiring notoriety as novelists, have been composed and published by different foreigners in regard to the Mexican nation. The impressions received during a rapid excursion of pure amusement, without making any longer stay in the various towns, than the time required to repack their valise and continue on a journey of useless results; the isolated facts that are observed in every society in contradiction to general rules, and a disposition to judge events without a proper examination and careful study, are not sufficient to obtain a complete knowledge of any class of people, and much less to authorize such impressions through the medium of the press. The works of similar writers, in misleading the conceptions of the public, conspire against the real utility of general information, as their ideas (in direct opposition to those given to the world by such profound observers as Humboldt, Burkart, Sartorius and Jourdanet,) cannot convey any instruction to our intelligence, but only dispose the mind to receive the impressions produced by the novel.

The scarcity of the population of Mexico in comparison to its large extent of territory; the unrivalled geographical position of the country, between the two great Oceans, the fertility and topographical advantages of its lands, which are adapted to every kind of productions and to the life of men of every clime, the docile character of its inhabitants, the admirable falls of water, particularly in the delightful temperate regions, with their perpetual streams, offer the highest inducements to the establishment of manufacturing and other enterprizes; the working of mines of precious metals and other useful mineral substances, the extraction especially of quicksilver and coal, and in short so many and so propitious gifts as those with which Nature has enriched Mexico, cause it to be one of the choicest countries in the world for colonization; but in order to attain this desirable object, it is requisite to make known those vital elements and fountains of wealth that yet remain unexplored, and with this purpose, the present work only leads the way to a series of publications destined for the information of those abroad, and written by Mexicans devoted to the prosperity of the Republic, and which will doubtless contribute to the development of so wished-for a result.

The first part of this work treats of the population in general and its classification; the second, of the immigration of the first settlers of Mexico; the third, of the ethnography and description of the different indigenous races, who are daily disappearing, and the last part is composed of the recapitulation detailing the numerical importance of these same people.

INDEX.

POLITICAL PART. Situation of the Republic, its extent and boundaries . . . . 9.
Government of the Republic . . . . 10.
Political division and population . . . . 12.
Occupations and manufactures. Agriculture . . . . . . 24.
Mining . . . . 25.
Arts and manufactures . . . . 28.
Trade . . . . 30.
Public instruction . . . . 33.
HISTORICAL PART. Immigration of the former settlers of Mexico. 41.
The Toltecs . . . . 43.
The Chichimecas . . . . 51.
The Nahuatlatas, Xuchimilcas, Chalcas, Tepanecas, Acolhuas, Tlahuicas and Tlaxcaltecas . . . . 53.
Aztecs or Mexicans . . . . 55.
ETHNOGRAPHICAL AND DESCRIPTIVE PART. General considerations regarding the indigenous race . . . . 61.
Ethnographical tables . . . . 65.
I Mexican family . . . . 67.
II Sonora or Opata–Pima family . . . . 70.
III Comanche–Shoshone family . . . . 75.
IV Texian or Coahuilteca family . . . . 78.
V Keres–Zuñi family . . . . 80.
VI Mutzun family . . . . 81.
VII & VIII Guaicura and Cochimi–Laimon family . . . . 82.
IX Seri family . . . . 83.
X Tarasca family . . . . 84.
XI Zoque–Mixe family . . . . 92.
XII Totonaca family . . . . 93.
XIII Mizteco–Zapoteca family . . . . 98.
XIV Pirinda or Matlaltzinca family . . . . 104.
XV Maya family . . . . 105.
XVI Chontal family . . . . 112.
XVII Families originating from Nicaragua . . . . 114.
XVIII Apache family . . . . 116.
XIX Othomi family . . . . 119.
RECAPITULATION. Numerical distribution of the indigenous families. Report on the races. Causes of their decline. 125.

GEOGRAPHICAL SITUATION OF THE REPUBLIC:

ITS EXTENT AND BOUNDARIES

THE territory of the Mexican United States embraces an extent of 9.343,470 square kilometres, comprised within 15° and 32° 42' of Latitude North and between 12° 21' Longitude East and 18° West of the capital of the Republic; or 86° 46' 8" and 117° 7' 8" West of Greenwich. On the North it is bounded by the United States of America, with which, the River Bravo forms the line of division, at three leagues from its mouth, from whence it continues in the direction of that river by the States of Tamaulipas, Coahuila and Chihuahua, up to the parallel of 31° 47' of latitude North, near to the town of Paso del Norte; from this point for one hundred miles in a straight line to the West; thence to the South, to parallel 31° 20' Latitude North; the same parallel continuing from this point to 111° of longitude West of Greenwich; from here in a right line to a point on the River Colorado, situated at 20 miles below the confluence of the Gila with the same river; and from thence up the river as far as where the boundary line meets between the two Californias. On the South East, it is bounded by the Republic of Guatemala, whose limits have not yet been geographically defined. On the East, the coasts of the Republic are bathed by the waters of the Gulf of Mexico, which extend themselves, without taking into account their development, 2,580 kilometres; of which 400 pertain to Tamaulipas, 640 to Vera Cruz, 190 to Tabasco, 360 to Campeachy and 990 to Yucatan. On the West, the coasts that are bathed by the waters of the Grand Ocean composing the Gulf of California, embrace a greater extent, or about 6,650 kilometres, and of these, Lower California measures from 2,900 to 3,000, Sonora 860, Sinaloa 510, Jalisco 500, Colima 160, Michoacan 130, Guerrero 460, Oaxaca 410 and Chiapas 220.

At the South Eastern part of Yucatan, the territory of Belize is situated, which is in possession of the English, in virtue of a permit for cutting timber. Its limits are stated in the treaty of peace entered into between the King of Spain and the King of Great Britain, signed on the 3rd of November 1783 and amplified on the 14th of July 1786. In these treaties, the rivers Hondo, Belize and Sibun appear as the limits.

GOVERNMENT OF THE REPUBLIC

THE government of the Republic is representative, democratic and federal. The capital of the nation, which is also that of the District, is the residence of the Supreme powers of the Federation, wich are distributed into Legislative, Executive and Judicial.—The Legislative power is composed of the general Congress, divided between the Chamber of deputies and that of the Senate. The members of the assembly of deputies are elected in their totality by Mexican citizens, every two years, one for each 40,000 inhabitants and for every fraction exceeding 20,000. The Senate is composed of two Senators for each State and two for the Federal District, the election being indirect in the first degree, and proceeding from the respective legislatures of the States.

The Executive power is deposited in one sole individual, denominated "The President of the Mexican United States," whose election is popular, and for a term of four years, he entering upon his duties on the first of December. The President has the power of appointing six Secretaries of State ; namely, for the Foreign Department, Home Department, Justice and Public Instruction, ("Fomento") or Public Works and Colonization, Finances and Public Credit, and War and Marine. The judicial power is constituted of the Supreme Court of Justice, and the District and Circuit Courts. The first is composed of eleven proprietary magistrates, four supernumeraries, one "fiscal" and one solicitor general. Their election is also popular, and for a period of six years.

The President of the Supreme Court is the Vice-President of the Republic.

The States of the Mexican Federation are free, sovereign and independent, in all that concerns their interior regimen, but united in conformity with the precepts of the Constitution founded upon the rights of man and social guarantees, sanctioned on the fifth of February 1857.

POLITICAL DIVISION AND POPULATION

THE present population of the Republic reaches the cipher of 9.495.157 inhabitants, distributed in the following manner:

		FRONTIER STATES.	
I	Sonora,		115,000
II	Coahuila,		104,137
III	Chihuahua,		190,000
IV	New Leon,		190,000
			599,137

		STATES ON THE GULF OF MEXICO.	
V	Tamaulipas,		140,000
VI	Vera Cruz,		520,000
VII	Tabasco,		95,597
VIII	Campeachy,		86,000
IX	Yucatan,		300,000
			1.141,597

		STATES ON THE PACIFIC OCEAN.	
X	Sinaloa,		200,000
XI	Jalisco,		980,000
XII	Colima,		65,827
XIII	Michoacan,		618,240
XIV	Guerrero,		325,000
XV	Oaxaca,		661,706
XVI	Chiapas,		195,000
			3.045,773

		CENTRAL STATES.	
XVII	Durango,		185,000
XVIII	Zacatecas,		414,000
XIX	Aguascalientes,		90,000
XX	San Luis Potosi,		525,110
XXI	Guanajuato,		900,000
XXII	Queretaro,		166,643
XXIII	Hidalgo,		427,340
XXIV	Mexico,		663,557
XXV	Morelos,		150,000
XXVI	Puebla,		700,000
XXVII	Tlaxcala,		122,000
			4.343,650
	District of Mexico,		340,000
	Territory of Lower California.		25,000
			9.495,157

The last reports from the State Governments have given the greater part of the data for the formation of the preceding census, but part of them not being of a very recent date, on account of some of the authorities not having presented the respective documents, from not being required to do so by their particular constitutions, I have found myself obliged to obtain the necessary information by means of calculation, taking for my basis, previous data and the changes in the population. The relations which affect the annual increase, vary in distinct parts of the Republic, owing to the differences of climate, elevation, topographical position of the places, dryness or humidity of the soil, and the abundance or scarcity of timber lands principally exercising their influence in the increment of the population, in the altitude and consequent pressure of the air. Doctor Jourdanet, in the work he so conscientiously published,*established three divisions, denominating them: upper table lands, intermediate region and lower region, considering the first as at an elevation of more than 2,000 metres, the second from 800 to 2,000 metres and the third from the level of the sea to 800.

Comparing the census of the year 1810 with that of 1858, Doctor Jourdanet considers the annual increase of population in 3.06 for each 1,000 inhabitants in the upper table lands, and in 6.50 in the lower and intermediate regions; and again comparing the data relative to 1838 and 1857, he obtains 8.57 for each 1,000 in the first named region and 9.84 in the second.

Imperfect as may have been the data that served as the basis of these calculations, statistical results, as Dr. Jourdanet observes, contradict the general belief as to the superiority of the life of man in the higher regions, to those of the intermediate ones. The results he obtained cannot be considered as entirely correct. The imperfection of the census, and particularly that of 1810; the war of independence; the epidemics; the revolutions that have agitated the Republic; the foreign wars and other perturbing causes, as also the situation of the towns in which the difference of height changes suddenly; and the climatological conditions of each one of the three regions referred to, are so many circumstances that make a perfect calculation impossible.

---
* Influence of the pressure of the air on the life of man. -- PARIS, 1875.

The more recent data, as a natural result of the advancement of the people and of more reliable statistics, and principally as a consequence of the state of tranquillity, which the Republic has enjoyed during the last seven years, and but slightly disturbed, offers most certainly a better basis for obtaining an annual report as to the increase of population. Whether comparison be made as to the census of distinct periods, in relation to certain localities, or whether they all be confronted together; in any way whatever, a result will be obtained, analogous to those acquired by Dr. Jourdanet, even although the numbers indicated by the reports be very different. Those that have reference to the latest data ought to be considered as approaching nearest to the truth, from the fact that they have been ascertained during a period that has not been interrupted by disturbances interfering with the natural increase of population. After having regularly observed this increase for the space of fifteen years, and comparing the latest data referred to, I have obtained 1.10 per cent of annual increase in the upper region and 1.85 per cent in the intermediate and lower countries.

The differences of dress, customs and language, in the Mexican Republic, make known the heterogeneousness of its population, which may be divided into three principal groups; viz, the white race and more direct descendants of the Spaniards, the mixed race and the Indian race.

The habits and customs of the individuals who compose the first division, conform in general to European civilization, and particularly to the fashions of the French with reminiscences of the Spaniards. Their national language is Spanish; French is much in vogue, whilst English, German an Italian are greatly extended.

The bases of public instruction of which I shall speak hereafter, are composed of literary and artistical classical works, a knowledge of the Latin and Greek roots, and the great principles of science in all its branches. To the latter group in general, belong the exercise of various professions, and the vital element of capital, which forms the firmest support of agriculture, the arts, mining enterprices and trade, for the development of which, the Republic maintains close relations with Europe and the United States. Existing these relations, as they really do exist, the unacquaintance as to our civilization in the old world, is incomprehensible, nor is it credible that some few books, written with inexactness and evil intention, should preponderate over the instructive pages and valuable conceptions emitted in good faith, by a Humboldt, a Burchart, a Sartorius or a Jourdanet. The works of many distinguished Mexicans are also deserving of praise, as they alone would suffice to make known the reality of our social status. The books that have been published in Europe, in regard to Mexico, well merit refutation from their misrepresentations, but as this is not the object of the present work, I shall only occupy myself with one publication, having tendences to defame the character of the Mexican ladies, — a most despicable trait,— when, for their brilliant qualities, both in social and in domestic life, they are entitled to the highest commendation. The conjugal happiness enjoyed by many foreigners united to Mexican women affords the most solemn contradiction that can be given to similar detractors.

Mr. Figuier, in his work of "The human races," reproduces an engraving from another European publication, which represents the type of a woman of the people, and not that of one of the principal ladies of Mexico, as he supposes. This type is taken from a correct photograph by Mr. Jules Michaud and is the same that I have copied in No. 1 of my collection, plate No. II. I have also represented the type of another woman of the lower class who appears in Mr. Figuier's work as the servant of the former. On comparing Mr. Michaud's photograph with the engraving shown in the work referred to, I have formed the conviction that there has been bad faith in its reproduction. In the photograph, which has been transferred in the number referred to, a woman is seen of an agreeable and lovely figure, and not with the characteristics of the negro race, as she appears in the adulterated plate of Mr. Figuier's work. Moreover, this gentleman, who, doubtless, has produced many recommendable works, would have done well in abandoning the routine of classifying the Mexican nation among the red-skins.

It is to be supposed that the thirst of speculation has

obliged the editors of similar writings, to excite curiosity, by presenting the most extravagant types, instead of those that in their equality with Europeans, would attract little or no special atention. Other works, such as those of Eyma and Chevalier, which recommend themselves by their elegance of style and just appreciations, tend but little, as an ultimate result, to enlighten their readers, being confined to the political object with which they were written. By these works it may be remarked that both the middling class as well as those of a higher position, in their style of dress, follow the French fashions, without any other alteration, than that which depends upon the time required by the Steamers to bring the plates and sketches of the latest changes.

As I have already mentioned, the nearest descendants of the Spaniards and those less mixed up with the native race in Mexico, belong by their complexion to the white race, for which reason their number, to-day, is more considerable than is supposed. The natural inclination of the mixed race to the habits and customs of their white brethren, as well as their estrangement from those of the natives, is the reason that many of them figure in the most important associations of the country, by their learning and intelligence, including in this large number, the worthy members of the middling classes. From this powerful coalition, the force of an energetic development naturally results, which is inimical to the increment of the indigenous race, not a few of the natives contributing to this fatal consequence, who by their enlightenment have ingressed into the body I have referred to, thereby founding new families with the habits and customs of the upper classes.

The white race is found to be specially concentrated in the larger centres of population, and is generally extended throughout the country, its individuals revealing in the towns, the large landed properties and the most humble villages, the social qualities that adorn them, by their politeness and agreeable manners, as well as by their hospitable character. If Mexican civilization is not known in Europe, the fault belongs to some of the foreign travellers, who have disdained to enter into relations with the intelligent classes of society.

Desiring to disseminate a thorough acquaintance with

Mexican society, such as it really is, I fix myself by preference on all those qualities that characterize it and are entirely unknown abroad, without disowning, notwithstanding, the defects it is subject to and which are inherent to all the communities of the world. The distinguished German, E. Sartorius, who resided for many years in the country, and was without doubt, one of the few well informed foreigners in all concerning the Republic of Mexico, in his interesting dissertation, "The importance of Mexico for German emigration," treats of the character of Mexicans, circumscribing their defects and vices to their true limits. This learned German, whose recent death we sincerely deplore, expresses himself in the following terms:

"Doubtless, there are many names for all the mixed races, according to their origin from white and black, olive and white, olive and black, etc., but these are entirely insignificant politically and socially. There cannot exist any doubt, but that the Caucasian race, by its intelligence and capacity are those that prevail in the country; and therefore, speaking in common, the population is divided into only two classes, namely: white and colored.

"In Mexico there is no slavery: every one who treads its soil is free, even though he may have lived in a state of bondage. All the inhabitants are free and equal before the law. Only by judicial sentence can men be deprived of their civil active rights. Every individual, without distinction of color, is eligible to public employs, etc. This is established solely by the constitution and is practiced. Hereditary titles and dignities are abolished.

"On examining how these two bodies are divided in society, we find that the white population forms the class that fills the first rank in intelligence and position.

"According to numerical proportion, they compose the smaller fraction, especially in the Southern part of the Republic, whilst in the Northern sections, the white race predominates. Since the independence of Mexico, the prerogative of being a Spaniard by birth has no political importance, and as there are no genealogical trees to show distinction of blood many consider themselves as pure creoles who are probably of a mixed race, but who from their color might readily pass for white people. It is for this reason that their number has increased to a million and a half. According to official data the number of Europeans reaches thirty thousand individuals.

"The character of the Mexican creole assimilates considerably to that of the Spaniard from whom he descends, although he possesses more of the vivacity of the Andalusians than the gravity of the Castilians or Gallegos. He is active, jovial, ardent and gay, although frequently careless and prodigal. In their social behaviour, the creoles, both well and poorly educated, have much natural politeness, and in their mode of life possess many private virtues that render them worthy of esteem. I must mention, particularly, the respect paid by children to their parents; their hospitality: their humane treatment towards their servants, who are considered as belonging to the family, and their protection of orphans. Immediately a child loses its parents, it is adopted by its godfathers, and if these should be wanting, a rivalry is excited between other families to shelter the abandoned creature."

The mixed race, like that of the whites, occupy in general the larger centres of population, where they apply themselves to mechanical arts or are engaged as servants; they are also found disseminated over the whole country, employing themselves in agricultural labors, in mining, in manufacturing, and in mule-driving. As we see, this race as a whole, constitutes the working population of the Mexican people. Their language is Spanish, intermixed with a multitude of provincial expressions, of very distinct and marked accents, and composed in a great part of words derived from the Indian dialects. The Catholic religion is that which predominates, but it must be observed that it is among this class of people that the Protestant sects principally acquire their proselytes. Sagacious, intelligent and with a special gift for imitation, this race is remarkable for the taste and perfect construction of its manufactures: in printing and book-binding; in carpenters and blacksmith's, work; in sculpture of stone and wood; in hat-making, boot and shoemaking, in the manufacture of cotton, woollen and silk stuffs, and to conclude, in all the mechanical arts, the workmen reveal their ability and intelligence. Among them, the first rudiments of well organized education are not unknown, such as reading and writing, and not a few have acquired other accomplishments as useful in the arts as serviceable to the citizen.

The desire of improvement in their social condition and in their education has developed itself amongst them, in a most remarkable manner; the idea of forming associations, (which in Mexico do not have as their object the interruption of public order, but fraternity and mutual benevolence,) has been already carried into effect by some of the societies of the working classes, in their late strikes. Not only in the larger cities, but in some of the second and third order, well regulated associations are being founded, at which the artisans congregate, in places chosen for the purpose, at times to attend lectures and to promote discussion upon some interesting subject, not even excepting matters of science, and on other occasions to hold evening parties with their families. Nearly all these societies have their libraries which contribute to their instruction, and others have established Schools and classes of declamation.

The same gentleman, Mr. Sartorius, to whom I have already referred, confirms what I have previously stated regarding the mixed race, and the good qualities of the Indians. The following are his words:

"It is in the mixed race ("mestizos") principally that we find the field-laborers and smaller cattle-raisers, called "rancheros," who form a very important and meritorious part of the population, and are the most robust, and constitute the mediocrity of the farming people. Proceeding from this class, we have the greater part of the miners, the large number of "arrieros" or mule-drivers, pedlars, artisans, servants of every kind in the city and in the country, the sailors and soldiers and the huntsmen. The Indians agree with them, much less than with the white people, and call them "*coyotl*," (a kind of jackal.) The Indians are much addicted to fermented drinks, whilst the others are partial to gambling, to which they give themselves up indiscriminately. In general the "mestizo" possesses many excellent qualities: he is quick and discreet, industrious, intelligent, faithful in his master's service, hospitable and attentive.

The number of negros and mulattos is limited; they are only found on the coasts, employed as artisans, fishermen and day-laborers.

Every one who has lived in Mexico for any length of time and has been in contact with all classes, ought to bear testimony that the people in general are good, acute, dexterous, laborious, ingenious and disposed to any improvement. When it be considered how little has been done or is doing to give them an adequate moral and intellectual education, we cannot avoid being surprised at the good fund of probity that prevails amongst all classes. I have lived for many years among the Indians and mixed race, and never have I enjoyed greater security in my person and in my property and interests, than during the period referred to. What could not be done in Europe is practised in Mexico without any fear, and that is to trust to a poor and barefooted day-laborer large sums of money, to be carried by him alone, a distance of many leagues, and it never occurs that the wretched Indian commits a breach of confidence. Such a vice is, up to the present, an exception."

The individuals belonging to the mixed race are vigorous, especially in the Northern parts of the Republic. Owing to their lively and ardent temperament, they are inclined to pleasure and to certain amusements which like bull-fighting, are fortunately disappearing, in virtue of the laws that govern Mexicans; but what particularly distinguishes the character of this race especially and of Mexicans in general, is their tenacious and strenuous resistance to submit themselves to force, and their docility in ceding to persuasion. If these qualities had been seasonably known in foreign countries, the European intervention would never have been resolved upon. It was to this race that belonged the greater number of those who rose against Spain and maintained a tremendous struggle until gaining the independence of the country.

In their public rejoicings and festivities, this race reveals its gay and cheerful character, giving way to every species of amusements; their field sports consisting in "coleaderos"

or chasing and throwing bulls by the tail, but without practising, in these cases, the acts of cruelty that are customary in the iniquitous spectacle of public bull fights ; but on the contrary the "rancheros" partake of this favorite diversion in order to display their dexterity in horsemanship and the use of the "lazo": then again they have their dances, which in the interior are of a distinct character from those of the coast, although, in all, the *"jarabe"* is one of the most attractive. In the 3rd group of plate II, the types of the people of Guadalajara are represented, one of the gayest of our populations, and who, with reason, presume to have no rivals in the rest of the cities of the Republic, for the grace and skill with which they execute this lively dance. The following notes will give an idea of the kind of music of the "jarabe." (See N° 1.)

The rhymes sung by those playing the instruments, suddenly interrupting the music of the "jarabe", are characterized by piquant and caustic ideas, frequently with allusion to some remarkable local or political event. The following music which is very popular in Mexico, will serve as a specimen: (See N° 2)

In the interior, in the country towns, as well as in the farming districts and mountain villages, the taste for music is exceedingly general, and here I must transcribe one of the most characteristic ballads: (See N° 3.)

On the coast, the dances called "de tarima" (a raised wooden floor) are of an original character, from the very moment of the invitation. This is carried out by means of loud detonations, which are repeated for the purpose of making known to the guests, (who are generally all the neighbours) the place of meeting. In the middle of a street, and but dimly lighted by the glimmering of a lantern, a "tarima" or wooden floor is placed, around which accomodations are prepared for the visitors. A harp, a guitar and a "jarana" (a guitar of small dimensions) are the instruments played, at whose first tones the couples ascend the "tarima" and prepare for dancing. The musicians play lively pieces, many of them adapted to pantomimic dances, but in general very exciting and sprightly, such as the *"jarabe"*. The gracefulness and dexterity of the dancers consist in keeping time, and in imitating the melodies of the music, with the soles of their feet. The verses abound in wit, satire and caustical inuendoes, whose pith and pointedness are increased by the humor of the singers, their mode of expression, and their real or intentional hypocrisy, causing the hilarity of the listeners. On intonating their songs, they affect the greatest serenity, and with a perfectly stoic indifference give vent to their racy and pungent verses, closing their eyes as if overcome by slumber. On many occasions, extemporary improvisations are provoked, frequently on a given subject, when considerable nonsense is sometimes interspersed with sparkling drollery.

The "jarochos" of Veracruz, represented in group the 1st of Plate III, are those who give the greatest zest to this class of diversions. For a specimen of their festive and joyful musical compositions, see note N° 4.

Among the same group may be seen a creole woman from the "mesa de Mitlatloyuca," and the method they have of carrying water.

As in all the rest of the Republic, the mixed race of Yucatan is remarkable for their jovial character. It is there that the festivities called "baquerías," acquire the stamp of real frankness. Before dancing commences, pretended matrimonial engagements take place, in order that each individual may know who is to be his companion whilst these diversions last. These apparent contracts, authorized by the head of the house or the most elderly person present, give rise to disputes, jealousies and reconciliations all equally feigned, each one of those aggrieved, making his complaints to the person representing the parish priest,

The "jarabe" (the music of which I have given under note No. 1) and other tunes, especially one called the "toro" or bull (piece No. 5) of a lively nature, produce an extraordinary animation among the persons assembled; the whole ending by an imitation of the movements of a bull-fighter, sometimes "capoteando" or dancing before the bull with a cloak and at others pretending to escape from his onsets. On the conclusion of the ball, all the couples seek the open air and proceed in an orderly manner to a place at some distance from the house, where a stake has been previously placed to which a young bull or heifer is tied.

A distinguished traveller, Mr. Stephens, portrays the impressions of his journey to Yucatan, in the most lively colors and particularly those he felt at a dance in Ticul. What attraction does a "mestiza" dance present to Mr. Stephens, enquires Mr. Nicoli in an article he published? What is this boisterous dance for the traveller? A fantastic diversion that excites the admiration and causes unspeakable rapture :—a woman or rather a sylph of an airy figure and more flexible than a reed, with a rich and pretty silk handkerchief carelessly thrown over her shoulders, a diminutive and exceedingly fine straw hat, scarcely touching the head and adorned with an infinity of ribbons forming a species of crown, a white dress embroidered, but so transparent that her fairy forms are seen exciting fascinating sensations and dreams of enchantment, her locks of matted hair tied with all the colors of the rainbow; here is a being that by her costume and grace might rival with a trastiberine of the October feasts at Rome.—Now if she plants herself in the centre of the saloon displaying that neat and diminutive foot that would be envied by a Thetis, what soul could resist —what heart would not kindle at similar allurements? With much reason Mr. Stephens was enchanted, and it is no wonder that it was with difficulty that he withdrew his sight from such voluptuous and graceful movements.

OCCUPATIONS AND CALLING OF THE MEXICANS.

AGRICULTURE.

THE Mexicans pertaining to the category I am referring to, are employed in agricultural labors, in working the mines, in mechanical arts and professions, and in various branches of manufacture, there now being established in the greater part of the States of the Republic, cotton, woollen, silk, earthenware, glass and paper factories, which will doubtless acquire greater importance in proportion to the depreciation of the value of silver in foreign markets. With regard to agriculture, which is the vital element in all countries, Mexico suffers from the scarcity of population, notwithstanding that the actual production is more than sufficient for the consumption ; and there are some articles such as coffee, timber, dye-woods, tobacco, vanilla, etc., which are exported in abundance. If all the country were populated, even in proportion to Guanajuato and its territory, the census of the Republic would reach 58.000,000 of inhabitants, and then agricultural products would be so much greater, that they would constitute an element of enormous wealth.

Within the territory of the Republic there are more than 5,700 " haciendas" (landed estates) and 13,800 farms ("ranchos") and not a few other locations of immense extent. The value assigned to landed property, based simply on its valuation for taxes, is 161.397,311 dollars, the real value of which without any serious error, may be calculated at double the amount or 322 millions of dollars. To be convinced that this calculation is not exaggerated, it will suffice to observe that in the amount named, each "hacienda" barely represents a value of $ 45,000 and each "rancho" of $ 5,000, without taking into account that of the streams, grazing lands, orchards and other rural property of less importance. The "maize" which is grown all over the territory, the wheat in the upper table-lands, the rice in the warm and damp sections, the coffee, vanilla, tobacco, sugar and cotton in the hot countries, and many other articles, among which may be mentioned the "agave Mexicano" with its abundant returns, constitute the principal branches of national agriculture, and it may be safely stated that the annual crops produce more than 100 millions of dollars. How immense would be the benefit to be derived by colonists employing their activity and intelligence in making such rich and extensive lands productive, under the influence of a delicious climate and in the midst of brothers and not of enemies, as it has been attempted to make believed abroad!

MINING.

THE metalliferous productions in the whole extent of the Republic are extremely rich and varied, for which reason this country has been reputed as essentially mineral. A considerable part of the laboring population is engaged in working the mines, in the reduction of the ores and in coining silver and gold, and this forms the first branch of our exportation. The want of enterprize, as a consequence of our scarcity of inhabitants, impedes the natural development of mining, as well as of agriculture and manufactures. The mineral districts that have been discovered since very remote periods, have produced immense amounts of money, and notwithstanding, it may be said that they are yet in their virgin state. The mines of Guanajuato which, without fear of contradiction, are those that have been the best worked and on the largest scale, still present enormous wealth. The soil of the State of Guerrero may be considered, according to the expression of one of our most celebrated mineralogists, as one extensive crust of silver and gold. In Sinaloa, the waters have submerged a rich treasure in the famous mine of "La Estaca." The States of Zacatecas, Sonora, Chihuahua, Durango, San Luis Potosi, Hidalgo, Mexico and Michoacan containt within their mountain ranges inexhaustible riches, and lastly the other States of the Mexican confederation, in every direction offer up to the assiduity of man an abundance of metalliferous deposits. Silver and gold ores are those that are principally worked in the mining regions, although other metals and mineral substances are found in great abundance, such as copper, iron, zinc, lead, magistral, antimony, arsenic, cobalt, amianthus and copperas. Sulphur is also met with in large quantities in many parts, and that of the mountain of Popocatepetl is considered as exhaustless. Salt mines are plentiful, such as those of the "Peñon Blanco" in San Luis Potosi ; those of the coast of Tamaulipas, the South of the Isthmus of Tehuantepec and the Islands of the Gulf of California. The lake of Texcoco and its adjacent lands possess an inestimable supply of carbonate of soda. In every State there exist splendid quarries of white and colored marble ; the alabaster at Tecali in the State of Puebla, has attracted great attention and may be advantageously compared for its beauty with the finest marble from the East.

Ways of comunication will hereafter be the most fruitful germen of commercial prosperity, by facilitating the working of the extensive coal-fields, platina and quick-silver mines existing in the asperities of the mountainous portions of the country. Among the precious stones, we have the opal of hues as varied and beautiful as those of Hungary, the turquoise, garnet, topaz, agate and amethyst, besides a very pure rock crystal. There is also a great variety of building stone.

The mineral districts that have been discovered in the Republic, up to the present, are very numerous, but they are in a great part paralized, for the causes referred to. Those that are actually working, according to the reports of the introduction of ores at the Assaying offices, are 117. The quantity of ore brought for assay in the period of one year amounts to 487,000 kilograms, of which 360,101 kilograms were reducible by the "patio" process, 99,330 by smelting and 27,569 by the barrel process, the whole representing a value of $ 19.100,178 15. The real mineral production is even greater than the amount stated, if we bear in mind that in consequence of the law permitting the free exportation of mineral ore, many of the mines do not send their products to the assay office, but export them directly.

The annual coinage is on an average 20 millions and a half of dollars, the whole amount coined since the establishment of the mints up to 1875 being $ 3,001.237,281 62, as follows:

	SILVER	GOLD	COPPER	TOTAL
In the Colonial period (1537 to 1821)	$2,082.260,657 14	$98,778,411 09	$12,800 35	$2,151.581,961 81
Since the Independence (1822 to 1875)	797,085,020 77	17,327,383 11	5,272,853 93	819,656,319 81
	$2,879.313,738 91	$116.105.794 11	$5,815,740 50	$3,001.237,281 62

ARTS AND MANUFACTURES.

THE favorable disposition shown by Mexicans towards the cultivation of the arts, has attained a considerable progress, if we reflect upon the backward state in which they were found in the early years of the independence. The last industrial Exposition, in spite of the non-concurrence of some of the most important well-doing States, has convinced Mexicans that they can, by themselves, supply all their necessities, without requiring luxury. The printing and lithography can place before the world books and illustrations, worthy of acceptance to bibliographers. Carved work and filigree work in gold and silver yield in little or nothing to similar productions from abroad. The carriages and household furniture made in Mexico, with the exception of silk stuffs, can compete in taste and solid workmanship with the best that can be imported from foreign countries. In the fine arts, both in painting as well as sculpture and architecture, our Academy of San Carlos, reputed by travellers to be the first in America, displays the progress they have acquired. Some of these works will be exhibited to the public at the Philadelphia Exposition. The fabrication of textures as well as all other manufactures has increased astonishingly. Several factories, sugar mills and distilleries are established in the States of Mexico, Puebla, Veracruz, Jalisco, Morelos, Guerrero, Tabasco, Oaxaca and Yucatan: earthenware is made in Guanajuato, Mexico and Puebla; in the State of Jalisco and in the Valley of Mexico there are various paper-mills; also some glass factories in Mexico and Puebla: cotton factories in the greater part of the States: silk-factories in Guanajuato, Queretaro and Mexico. The number of cotton factories in the Republic exceeds 70, the States that may be considered as manufacturing districts being those of Puebla, Jalisco, Queretaro, Mexico and Veracruz.

The data I have been able to acquire regarding these factories, will be seen in the following statement:

STATES.	FACTORIES.	Number of Spindles.	Number of Looms.	Pieces produced yearly.	Kilograms of yarn.	Kilo. of cotton consumed yearly.
Puebla.	Guadalupe.	2,100	48	12,500	43,723	92,049
	Santa Cruz	2,100	50	12,500	44,183	92,049
	Constancia.	3,780	90	22,500	79,530	165,687
	Economía	2,520	60	15,000	53,847	110,459
	Patriotismo.	8,500	200	50,000	174,893	368,197
	Beneficencia.	2,000	50	13,000	46,025	92,049
	Mayorazgo,	5,250	120	30,000	138,074	266,942
	De en Medio.	6,300	150	40,000	124,266	230,123
	Amatlan.	1,550	36	9,000	32,217	69,037
	Teja.	1,550	36	9,000	32,217	69,037
	Asuncion	2,100	50	15,000	46,025	92,049
	Independencia.	1,550	36	8,500	34,518	69,037
		39,300	926	237,000	849,518	1.716,715
Jalisco.	Prosperidad Jalisciense.	2.976	90	33,084	24.835	211,712
	Experiencia.	792	,,	,,	41,422	50,627
	Escoba	3,300	69	28,000	285,353	299,159
	Bellavista.	5,832	156	24,886	,,	138,073
	Jauja.	4,768	112	37,992	35,979	329,075
		17,668	427	123,962	387,589	1.028,646
Querétaro.	Hércules La Purísima.	22,000	680	350,000	1.150,615	1.380,739
District and State of Mexico.	Magdalena.	13,000	376	156,000	167,530	598,504
	Tlalpam.	13,000	450	150,000	165,689	603,106
	Tizapam.	9,000	176	135,000	105,303	516,394
	Miraflores.	7,000	262	108,992	46,046	372,799
	Abeja.	1,400	,,	..	..	,,
	Colmena	4,300	,,	,,	..	,,
		47,700	1,264	549,992	484,568	2.090,803
Veracruz.	Cocolapan.	7,000	400	75,000	415,467	429.870
	Libertad.	2,000	81	1.944	118,973	,,
	Victoria.	600	22	,,	133,471	,,
	Industria Jalapeña.	4,028	57	19,992	124,266	,,
	Lucas Martin	3,984	..	..	124.266	161,081
	Rosario.	1,584	..	..	..	138,073
	Probidad.	1,056	,,	,,	..	67,195
		20,254	560	96,936	914,543	796,219

Besides "mantas" (cotton domestics) in some of these establishments and in other special factories, worked by the most improved machinery, other goods are manufactured, such as diapers, madapollans, muslins, bed ticks, satteens and linen drills, fine and coarse carpeting, counterpanes, fine spun and ordinary kerseymeres, baize and other textures. In Puebla, Mexico, Jalisco and several places in other States, there are silk spinning and twisting factories, whose products, from the fact of the raw material being of superior quality, are preferred to those from abroad, amongst them, stuffs for ladies dresses, handkerchiefs, scarfs ("pañosdereboze") and every kind of lace and fancy trimmings. In Mexico are also manufactured kid gloves, cotton lace and hosiery, braces, cotton and woollen gloves, tape, embroidered ribbons and other articles of a similar kind, which with the exception of the first named, form a peculiar branch of industry among the Indians and some of those condemned to prison.

Gold and silver lace work and wire-drawing is carried on in a large scale, in every branch of this department, and of a superior style of workmanship and excellent quality. To conclude, in every town of any importance, there may be observed a great advancement in arts and manufactures.

COMMERCE.

THE Mexican United States maintain mercantile relations with England, France, the United States of America, Germany, Spain and the Island of Cuba, Belgium, Italy, Central America, the United States of Colombia, and the Equator.

According to the annual Reports the value of the importations may be estimated at 29.000,000 of dollars, in the following form:

Cotton and cotton goods,	$ 10.500,000
Groceries, wines and spirits,	5.000,000
Articles free of duty,	3.300,000
Hardware and ironmongery,	2.100,000
Miscellaneous,	2.000,000
Linen and hemp goods.	1.400,000
Woollen goods,	1.400,000
Mixed goods,	1.400,000
Silks,	1.000,000
Earthenware, porcelain, glass and crystal ware.	600,000
Drugs and Chemicals,	300,000
Total.	$ 29.000,000

This amount is imported from the following countries:

England,	$ 10.200,000
United States of America,	7.500,000
France,	4.780,000
Germany,	3.800,000
Spain and the Island of Cuba.	1.400,000
United States of Colombia.	1.200,000
Central America,	100,000
Italy, Belgium, and American Republics..	20,000
	$ 29.000,000

The exportation amounts to 31.000,000 of dollars, as follows:

Gold and silver coin,	$ 24.000,000
Ores and minerals,	1.800,000
Carried forward.	$ 25.800,000

Brought forward .	$ 25,800,000
Hides and skins in general, . . .	1,800,000
Henequen, Ixtle and cordage,	1,000,000
Timber and dyewoods, . .	1,000,000
Coffee, . .	600,000
Vanilla, .	400,000
Cochineal, ...	300,000
Cattle,	200,000
Tobacco,	150,000
Orchilla, .	130,000
Fine pearls, ...	110,000
Caoutchouc or Indian-rubber,	100,000
Sarsaparrilla, . .	90,000
Wool, ...	90,000
Sole and upper leather,	80,000
Indigo, .	80,000
Jalap root, ...	80,000
"Coquito" (a small cocoanut), .	50,000
"Frijol" (beans),	40,000
Cotton, ...	30,000
Mother-of-pearl, . .	25,000
Starch, .	25,000
Wheat, ...	20,000
Other agricultural and industrial productions. .	100,000
	32,300,000

These exports are made to the following countries:

England, to the amount of	$ 12,550,000
United States of America, .	12,000,000
France, . .	5,000,000
Germany, ...	1,500,000
Spain and the Island of Cuba, .	800,000
Central America, ...	100,000
Italy and Belgium, .	50,000
	$ 32,000,000

PUBLIC INSTRUCTION

As the grade of civilization of any country is principally to be inferred from its development in public instruction, I cannot close this chapter without explaining the progress made in this important matter. Señor Don José Diaz Covarrubias, the present Sub-secretary of the Department of Justice and Public Instruction, has just written and issued to the public a luminous book under the title of "Public Instruction in Mexico," in which abound the most conscientious remarks, demonstrating the increment acquired day by day in this element of such vital importance to universal progress.

The principle of obligatory education having been admitted, it is now in force in the greater part of the States of the Republic, penalties having been decreed for those who contravene the law and rewards for those who voluntarily observe the same, a stimulus which cannot fail to contribute towards the accomplishment of so praiseworthy a determination. Primary instruction in the schools of the Republic consists of the following branches : Reading, writing, Spanish grammar, arithmetic, tables of weights and measures, morality and good manners, and moreover in the girls' schools needle-work and other useful labors. In some of the States the study of geography, national history and drawing are also obligatory, whilst in the schools that are not supported by the Government, notions of algebra and geometry, elements of general and natural history, ornamental and lineal drawing and the French language, are taught.

The number of primary schools in the whole of the Republic reaches 8,103 instead of 5,000 that existed in the year 1870. Of the number referred to, according to the work of Señor Diaz Covarrubias, 603 are supported by the State governments, 5,240 by the municipal authorities, 378 by private corporations or individuals, 117 by the Catholic clergy, besides 1,581 private establishments that are not gratuitous and 184 not classified. These schools are attended by 350,000 scholars of both sexes.

Secondary instruction, as well as professional education, are under the charge of the State, with subjection to the programmes established by the law which prescribes as a mandate the liberty of education and professions.

In the Republic there are 105 establishments of secondary and professional instruction, in the following form:

BRANCHES OF EDUCATION.

Number of establishments.		Number of scholars.
1	Special preparatory school in the city of Mexico — Mathematics, geography in all its branches, physics, chemistry, natural history, logic, and moral literature, professorship, ornamental and lineal drawing and the French and English languages. .	5,173
19	Civil colleges of jurisprudence. — Laws of nature, Roman, national, constitutional, administrative, international and marine laws and political economy. . . .	771
20	Schools of medicine and pharmacy and all the branches concerning apothecaries, physicians and surgeons.	454
10	Schools for engineers.—Descriptive and analytic geometry, topography & hydraulics, algebra, infinitesimal computation, mechanics, practical geodesy and astronomy, applied chemistry, mineralogy, geology, construction of roads, rail-roads, bridges and canals; mechanical, architectural and topographical drawing	251
50	Carried forward	6,649

Number of establishments.		Number of scholars.
50	Brought forward.	6,649
2	Naval schools.—All concerning this branch.	13
3	Commercial schools. — Arithmetic, mercantile correspondence, book-keeping, geography and statistics, political economy, mercantile and maritime law, knowledge of merchandize and languages.	500
3	Academies of arts and sciences.—Spanish language, laws of the country, arithmetic, algebra, geometry, trigonometry, drawing and modelling, lineal and mechanical draughting, physics and notions of chemistry and mechanics, choral singing and various arts.	500
2	Agricultural schools.—Public health, zoology, physics and applied chemistry, natural history, descriptive geometry, and topography, veterinaryship, anatomy, etc.	83
2	Academies of fine arts. — Drawing, painting, sculpture and engraving. . . .	700
2	Conservatories of Music and Declamation.—All the matters annexed to the art, from the first scale to harmony and composition, arithmetic, Spanish grammar, French and Italian, geography and history, declamation, acoustics and phonography, physiology and treatment of the voice and hearing, study of the ancient and modern stage and dramatic literature, prosody and poetry, history of the middle and modern ages, mythology, esthetics and fencing.	637
1	Military College.—Besides all the preparatory studies, military science in all its branches.	200
65	Carried forward.	9,282

Number of establishments.		Number of scholars.
65	Brought forward.	9,282
24	Conciliary Seminaries supported by the Catholic clergy.—Latin grammar, logic, metaphysics, ethics, mathematics, geometry and in some establishments chemistry and natural history, modern languages, notions of Greek, theology and jurisprudence, canonical and moral law. .	3,800
1	Blind school.—Reading and writing by special methods, Spanish grammar, arithmetic (theorical and practical), universal geography and geography and history of Mexico, notions of geometry and astronomy, French, morality, vocal and instrumental music, printing, book-binding, carpenter's work, shoemaking and turning.	40
1	Deaf and dumb school.—Spanish language, written especially by means of a manual alphabet, catechism and religious principles, elements of geography and general and national history, arithmetic, horticulture and gardening for the boys, needle-work and embroidery for the girls, book-keeping and drawing. . . .	24
14	Secondary schools for girls—Mathematics, cosmography, geography, domestic medicine, history and chronology, book-keeping, domestic economy and duties of woman in society, natural, figured and ornamental drawing, manual labors, horticulture and gardening, music, the French and Italian languages . . .	1,663
105		14,809

Adding these results to those obtained in respect to primary instruction, the following will be the data acquired: 8,208 educational establishments with 364,809 pupils.

Altogether these establishments are attended with the following annual expenses:

Primary gratuitous school, supported by the authorities.	$ 1.632,436
Private schools, by individuals.	1.188,168
Secondary and professional schools, by the authorities.	1.100,000
Total.	$ 3.920,604

The number of professors and employees in public instruction is 8,770.

Annexed to the establishments referred to there are 8 model schools.

285,509 males and 79,300 girls receive instruction, which proportion is not to be wondered at if we bear in mind that a great number of girls are educated in their own houses, for which reason there are no statistics in regard to them.

There are 20 public libraries containing in the whole 236,000 volumes, and private libraries containing from 1,000 to 8,000 works are innumerable; and there are some with as many as 20,000 and collections of manuscripts and books upon history and travels, literature, law, biography, eloquence, encyclopedias, classic authors, mathematics, physical sciences and antiquity relating to America, Asia, Egypt and Nubia.

The most remarkable museums of the Republic are those of antiquities in Mexico, Campeachy, Puebla and Merida:

Those of paintings in Mexico, Oaxaca and Puebla:

Those of natural history in Mexico and Guadalajara.

The National Museum of Mexico, to which is annexed that of natural history, contains a rich collection of Mexican antiquities, hieroglyphics, manuscripts, arms, utensils, idols, jewels and every species of ornaments. The Museum of Natural History at the Mining College, now the School of Engineers, is composed of two cabinets; in the first there is a well classified collection of geological specimens and another of zoology, which contains a large assortment, consisting principally of birds and insects; in the second are found two collections of minerals from Europe and Mexico, arranged according to the chemical-mineralogical system of Berzelius, followed by the work that the learned professor Don Andres del Rio wrote for the use of the students of the school referred to.

The Academy of San Carlos is one of the most notable institutions of the city of Mexico. This edifice contains several galleries where numerous original and valuable paintings are to be admired. Among those that most excel for their merit are the following: The seven virtues from the Lombardian school, a painting attributed to Leonardo de Vinci; Saint John of God, by Murillo; the widow Queen by Carreño, three paintings from the school of Leonardo de Vinci; the Olympic games by Charles Vernet; an episode of the Deluge by Coglieti; the supper at Emmaus by Zurbaran; Saint Jerome by Alonso Cano; Saint Sebastian attributed to Van Dycke: a virgin by Pietro de Cortona; another virgin by Perugino; Saint John the Baptist from the Spanish school and another by Ingres; an odelisque woman and Armenian bishop by Decaen; four large pictures of the Sevillian school; one of the Venetian school attributed to Paul Verone's: two oval paintings representing Saint Barbara and Saint Catharine by Guido Reni; four large classical landscapes by Markó, other works of Podesti and Silvagni and several of the Flemish and Dutch schools.

In the other saloons are to be seen the paintings of some of the most proficient students of the Academy, amongst which attention is principally attracted to the Saint Charles Borromeo by Piña; a Christ and Abraham's sacrifice by Rebull; Jesus Christ journeying to the village of Emmaus, by Sagredo; the captivity of the Hebrews and Noah's ark by Ramirez; Cristopher Colon before the Catholic Sovereigns, by Cordero; the Angel at the Sepulchre, by Monroy; Dante and Virgil by Flores, etc.; the most of these artists being pupils of Mr. Clavé, who on his departure for Europe left us a grateful memento, in his magnificent painting "Crazy Queen Jane" which appears among the other works referred to.

To conclude, some of the saloons are embellished with very remarkable paintings by ancient Mexican artists, such as Cabrera, Aguilera, the Juarez family, Ibarra, Arteaga, Vallejo, Echave and others.

In the Republic there exist 73 institutions dedicated to the cultivation of arts and sciences, of which 29 are scientific, 21 literary, 20 artistical and 3 of a mixed character.

In the year referred to in the work of Señor Diaz Covarrubias (1874) there where 168 publications, of which 18 were scientific, 9 literary, 2 artistical, 26 religious and 118 political; those for which a copyright had been taken out according to law, being 117. Of this number, 104 were original works on science and literature, 4 translations and 9 artistical, but it must be remarked that only a minority of authors apply for the privilege of copy-right.

HISTORICAL PART

IMMIGRATION

OF THE ANCIENT POPULATORS OF MEXICO

No one, up to the present, has drawn aside the veil that conceals the history of the populators of Mexico, previous to the Toltecs. The ruins of ancient edifices of a growing importance, met with from the North to the South, and the distribution of dialects in this part of the American continent, reveal a series of immigrations, that manifest in my opinion both the successive arrivals of certain tribes in search of lands adapted to their purposes, and the places where they definitely fixed their residence, constituting themselves into communities. Neither in America nor in Europe does either history or tradition discover the origin of their first populators. In the New Continent as well is in the old one, the remains of grand monuments are found demolished by the lapse of centuries, which only serve to indicate the perseverance of the ancient and unknown generations. What has been revealed to us by the magnificent ruins of Palenque and Comalcalco in Chiapas and Tabasco — by those of Uxmal and Chichen–Itza in Yucatan and those of Mitla in Oaxaca? Only the existence of former and occult generations, very superior in civilization to those of which history speaks to us.

Various historians, basing themselves on the interpretation of the monumental hieroglyphics and those of the indigenous papyrus, have attributed the origin of the races that populated the rich regions of Anahuac to seven families that immigrated successively from North America, all speaking one common language, the Nahuatl or Mexican; but history neither reveals the primitive derivation of those races, nor does it open up the mystery of the multiplicity of tongues and their dialects of so diverse a character.

According to the descriptive and comparative tables of Pimentel, none of the 108 languages which he has classified have any analogy to the Asiatic tongues, nor even to Othomi, which from consisting almost entirely in monosyllables and from its construction, was thought to be similar to the Chinese.

Notwithstanding, the identity of the language of the Esquimaux indicates the communication betwixt Asia and America, a circumstance, in my idea, which is demonstrated in the form of our ancient monuments and the art of their constructions. The "tumulos" or sepulchres—according to Sir John Lubbock in his work "Prehistoric man"—are found scattered over all Europe from the Atlantic coasts to the Ural mountains and covering a great part of the immense steppes of Asia from the Russian frontiers to the Pacific and from the plains of Siberia to those of Hindostan. In a similar manner, monuments of a like nature are found disseminated from the banks of the Gila to those of Usumacinta and from the shores of the Atlantic to those of the Pacific, the pyramids on this side, like those on the other, displaying the most admirable development of the same idea.

In my "Essay of comparison between the Egyptian and the Mexican pyramids," I did not call attention solely to the form of the monuments, but more particularly to their specialities and details both interior and exterior, and from their undeniable analogy I deduced the identity of artistic knowledge between one and the other people, but without wishing that from my conclusions the inference should be drawn of the Egyptian origin of the first populators of Mexico, as some have pretended to attribute to me, from simply reading the title of my work.

If we carefully examine the color of the skin, the configuration of the cranium and the features of the individuals of the Tartar race and the Mexican race, we shall find such a similarity between them that we can scarcely avoid inclining our opinion towards the belief, already somewhat generalized, that the latter descended from some of the former. Perhaps a really physiological study in this respect might throw some light on our hallucination.

I do not pretend to adduce these arguments with the view of convincing those who entertain contrary opinions to mine in regard to the origin of the primitive American races; the object by which I am guided is solely to demonstrate the obscurity of history and the distance that separates us from the manifest triumph of one of many conjectures.

With the view of presenting the greatest amount of data respecting the population of the Republic, and treating of the indigenous race, as unfortunate as it is deserving of an attentive study, it may be deemed proper to refer to some of the ancient historical notions, if only with the object of learning their origin.

The ancient history of Mexico commences with annals of the Toltecs; nevertheless it is believed that the country was inhabited previously by a wild people, amongst whom the "Olmecas" and "Xicalancas" and even the "Othomies" have been cited, as being considered among the very first inhabitants of the Mexican territory.

The hierogryphical inscriptions found amongst the ruins of the ancient edifices, which are generally characterized by their pyramidical form, have not even revealed the epochs of the construction of these monuments, nor the nations to which they belonged. As the former Mexicans were ignorant of the existence of any tribes previous to that of the Toltecs, the construction of the pyramids of Teotihuacan, Papantla and Cholula was attributed by them to the latter, whilst some historians ascribed them to other nations of greater antiquity. If therefore, history teaches nothing certain in regard to those monuments, as of much less antiquity, how can we avoid being at fault on contemplating the magnificent structures of Mitla, Palenque and Uxmal, which for their style, solidity and decorations excite well merited admiration and profound curiosity?

The Toltecs, if we are to judge by the statement of Ixtlilxochitl, were informed as to the creation of the world, the deluge, the building of the tower of Babel and the confusion of tongues. They held as a fact that the world had been destroyed three times and regenerated on an equal number of occasions, denominating each destruction as an "age" or darkening of the sun; the first catastrophe happening with the deluge, which they called "sol" or epoch of the waters — the second was by a hurricane, which they called "sol" or epoch of the wind, and the third by an earthquake to which they gave the name of "sol" or epoch of the earth, and lastly awaited the complete destruction of the world by fire.

On the Toltecs being expelled from their country, *Huehuetlapallan*, a place situated, according to Humboldt, towards the North West Coast of America, near 42° of Latitude North, they commenced their peregrination towards the South, in the year 596 of the vulgar era, led by their chiefs, and stationing themselves at various places and founding towns and cities, but without meeting for some time with an appropriate spot for their purposes. After more than a century of wandering, they arrived at Tollancinco, where they remained for 20 years, and founded the city of Tollan, which was the metropolis of their nation.

According to some writers, Tula, under the name of *Manhe-mi* already existed, and owes its rebuilding and its new name to the Toltecs, and the same occurred with the pyramids of Teotihuacan, which site was chosen by them for their religious ceremonies. The annals of this nation, then preponderating by its institutions and civilization, show that the place of their departure was at the city of *Tlachicatsincan* in the Huetlapallan country and that they effected their immigration, sailing by the Gulf of California and the coasts of Jalisco, until they reached Tochtepec on the borders of the Pacific.

According to the notices of Ixtlixochitl, on the Toltecs founding their monarchy, there already existed in the regions of Panuco and Huexotla, a savage tribe of the "Chichimecas," to whose chief they addressed themselves, soliciting a prince of that race to be elected as their king ; a flattering proposal by which the Toltecs hoped to secure themselves against the ferocious instincts of that barbarous people.

The same *Ixtlilxochitl* in another part of his history relates that the first king was chosen from among the Toltecs, and this is the most probable. The catalogue of the Toltec kings began with *Chalchihuetlanetzin* ("precious stone") in the year 667 of the vulgar era, and it was then that the law of succession commenced to rule designating the period of 52 years for each reign, the same law providing that if the monarch should die before the expiration of that term, a Republican government should be adopted for the time wanting, on the conclusion of which the legitimate successor should take charge of the destinies of the country.

It is a remarkable fact that all the Toltec monarchs completed the time fixed by law, with the exception of *Mitl*, whose reign was prolonged for another seven years, in virtue of the meritorious conduct and good qualities that adorned him.

On the death of the first king at nearly completing the fifty-two years, he was buried with all his insignias, the highest honors being paid to him.

In 719, Ixtliquechahuac or Ixacateclatl, as the legitimate successor, came to the throne. During his reign he continued the aggrandizement of the nation and was succeeded by prince Huetzin. In 1771, a little before the death of Ixtlilquechahuac, the astrologist Huetmatzin in his latter days collected in a large volume which was called the Teoamoxtli or divine book, all the rites, sacrifices and ceremonies of the Toltec people, the laws, maxims and sentences, the catalogue of kings and potentates and the astrological, artistic and scientific rules ; in one word, all the prosperous and adverse events, forming in this way the history of this great people, whose ruin he also predicted.

At the death of Huetzing (823) his son Totepeuh inherited the throne, his reign being remarkable for the peace and tranquillity enjoyed by the nation. Huetzin was succeeded by prince Necarxoh (875) and the latter by his son Mitl, the wisest of the Toltec kings, during whose dynasty the monarchy reached its greatest eminence. Enlightened and prudent, he dictated memorable laws and extended his authority to a very great distance; many villages, towns and cities were founded in his time, among which Teotihuacan (the place of adoration) which already existed, excelled the most, and being as it was the grand sanctuary of the Toltecs, it surpassed Tula in the grandeur of its temples, monuments and power. Teotihuacan was not only renowned for its edifices and extent, but also for its lofty pyramids, of which the largest was dedicated to the Sun and the smallest to the Moon, and perhaps the innumerable "tlateles" to the stars, if we consider the emblematic character of the people we refer to. These monuments, as I have already mentioned in another article, were in my opinion mausoleums and altars.

To counterpoise the supremacy that Teotihuacan had acquired over the capital, Mitl raised the magnificent temple of "la Rana" goddess of the waters, enriching its interior with ornaments of gold and precious jewels, and with the image of the goddess, made from an emerald. In Tollocan palaces were erected whose prepared stone represented, by means of hieroglyphics, the most remarkable events in the Toltec history. Palaces of an analogous style were built in Cuanahuac and other places, to which his dominion extended.

The Toltecs excelled in arts and sciences, and were so skilful therein, that many interpret the word toltec by artist, although the probability is that it means a native of Toltan. They worked both in gold and silver, making very curious articles from these metals; they carved the hardest rocks and polished precious stones. They also excelled in the sciences as proved by their astronomical labors, which gave them for result the exact computation of time, which was qualified by the distinguished astronomer Laplace, as original. They divided the year into eighteen periods of twenty days adding other complementary five days called (nememteni) or useless, this completing the solar year of 365 days; but as this exceeded the period of 365 days, by a little less than six hours, they formed an age of 52 years which they called *Huilimolpia*, bundle or link of years, and the age or century (*Huehuetilixtli*) of 104 years, adding thereto 25 days, hence resulting a difference of only one day in each 538 years.

Agriculture was prosperous, the Toltecs dedicating themselves principally to the cultivation of maize, chile, beans and other products, as well as to cotton which gave them good returns. The women spun and wove domestics, plain, twilled and quilted, and with colored patterns and figures.

The Toltecs were very intelligent in architecture and constructed their buildings with cut stones, packed at times one above another and at others set in mortar ; they perpetuated their annals by means of hieroglyphic characters, and finally in their laws, their habits and customs, they exhibited an advanced state of civilization.

In their religious ceremonies, they excluded human sacrifices, with the exception of those they performed in honor of *Tlatotl*, the God of waters, whom they worshipped on the summit of one of the highest mountains of the Sierra Nevada, to the East of Texcoco ; and that made to *Tonacatecuhtli ;* offering up to the first six maidens, and to the second a criminal who was broken to pieces by the projecting points of revolving stones.

The laws prohibited polygamy and decreed that the monarchs could not contract a second marriage ; and courage was as much admired in the men as modesty in the women.

A community which, like that of the Toltecs, based their stability on the observance of the law, as shown by their customs and the legitimate succession of their kings, could not be otherwise than prosperous and powerful.

Wisdom and prudence guided Mitl during his reign, and as an acknowledgement of such commendable qualities, the law was broken for the first time, and he continued on the throne to the day of his death, which happened 7 years after the expiration of the 52 years, and for the same merits, the widow queen Huihtlaltzin continued in power (year 986) with the aquiescense of her son Tecpancalzin.

On the death of queen Huihtlaltzin, four years afterwards,

(year 990) her son, the prince, held the reins of government, assisted by the nobility, but during his sway, the decline of the monarchy had its beginning.

A noble Toltec, called Papantzin, had discovered the method of extracting the juice from the "maguey" (agave Americano), and anxious to make his sovereign a present of that liquor, he with this purpose, made his daughter accompany him,—a noble maiden as lovely as her name, as she was called "the flower" (Xochitl). The lady presents herself and offers the beverage to the king, which pleased the sovereign exceedingly, not so much for the present as for the beautiful personage that brought it. He immediately conceived a violent passion for her and preoccupied himself solely in the contemplation of a plan to obtain the sinister ends, he desired. He took leave of the father and the daughter, but requesting them to repeat their favor, and intimating that on again doing so, it should be by the captivating Xochitl alone. She returned once more to the royal palace, but never to go back to her home. Seduced by the praises and offers of the monarch, she was prevailed upon to accede to his importunities and resign herself to live in the place of recreation, assigned to her by the king, who to screen his proceedings sent to say to Papantzin that wishing to unite his daughter to a king, one of his vassals, he had placed her under the care of a matron to give her a proper education. Some time passed over, when either from suspicion or from a desire to see his daugther, Papantzin resolved to seek her place of abode. After many enquiries and some bribery, he attained his object, and was introduced to some gardens where the lady was just at that moment, with an infant in her arms. Not approving of the disloyalty of his king, he addressed his daughter in these words: "*Has the king by chance, placed you here to play with children?*" Ashamed and tremulous, she confessed her weakness, and the noble Papantzin decided immediately on presenting himself to the king, demanding satisfaction for this affront. The following day, on Tecpancaltzin's listening to the conplaint of the old man, he consoled him by promising that he would not take a wife to himself, and that the son of Xochitl (who had received the name of Meconetzin or son of the "maguey") should inherit him. On the expiration of the term of the fifty two years of his reign, Tecpancaltzin fulfilled his promise, by having his natural son Meconetzin sworn in as king, who took the name of Topiltzin, and became the apple of discord in the Toltec kingdom.

The reign of this prince was made remarkable by the excellence of his government in the earlier years, by his dissipation and dissolute life in those following and by the energetic and appropriate measures he dictated ultimately, with the view of redeeming his faults. His disorderly conduct contaminated all classes of society and libertinage was such, that the priests in spite of their vows of chastity, lived publicly with some of the principal women : vice and the greatest scandal reigned every where, a state of disorder which was rapidly precipitating the nation towards an abyss, in the same degree that industry, labor and respect for the law, had previously flourished in all their splendor.

To this commencement of the inevitable decay of the people, other calamities followed as a just punishment of their crimes: at times the heavens sent down heavy rains that inundated the lands and destroyed the crops, and at others they were deprived of water, so that a frightful drought joined to the burning rays of the sun ruined the harvests and even the grain that had been stored in the granaries.

To crown their misfortunes, the lords of Xalisco, of the same race, alleging rights to the throne of Toltan and believing the law to have been violated by the exaltation of Topiltzin, invaded the possessions of this monarch's dominion with a large army. Neither the friendly expressions of the noble ambassadors sent to meet them by the king, nor the rich presents which, in his name, they offered them, sufficed to make the invaders desist from their intention, but on the contrary they continued their march until they penetrated the precincts of Tollan.

The persuasive conduct observed by Topiltzin, towards the monarchs of Xalisco, with the view of inducing them to abandon their undertaking, was fruitless, nothing more being procured from their tyrannical pretensions than a truce of ten years, which was conceded in order that preparations might be made for defense. This concession is not to be wondered at from a race that esteemed bravery and loyalty in all their worth. This compact gave as a first result the immediate withdrawal of the invading forces.

On the conclusion of the time stipulated, which was not misspent by the illustrious Topiltzin, he prepared for war, and posted his troops advantageously and selected the plains of Tultitlan as his headquarters. The enemy's hosts had scarcely borne in sight, when the advanced guard of the Toltec army rushed to attack them. The first battle was commenced, giving rise to a series of sanguinary struggles that lasted three years, the Toltecs, in the midst of all, sometimes conquerors and sometimes vanquished, displaying unheard of traits of bravery. The first division of the army having been completely routed, Topiltzin advanced with the aged Tecpancaltzin, at the head of their forces, the lovely Xochitl leading the ladies, who like a body of amazons, were also prepared for the combat. One and the other of the disputants rush to the struggle with the greatest bravery and courage ; the presence of their sovereigns animates and inspires the warriors who with their unerring arrows spread death and desolation on all sides, and even the ladies themselves and the women of the soldiers, imitating the example of queen Xochitl, penetrate into the midst of the heat of the battle, and fight hand to hand with the enemy's men. The battle lasts for three consecutive days and nights without suspension of hostilities, but not without the enemy's receiving fresh reinforcements, while the Toltecs were not aided by any new warriors. The forces of the latter becoming exhausted by so desperate a struggle, the enemy's superiority rose in proportion, and they gradually gained ground. At last, the victory was decided in favor of those of Xalisco, and the Toltec army having dispersed, took refuge in the mountains and lakes, only a small body of the army remaining which commenced its retreat, led by its two kings and queen Xochitl. This gallant army, closely persecuted and always resisting, reached Xaltocan ; from thence passed to Teotihuacan, and afterwards proceeded towards the mountains of the South by Totolapan. The king Tecpancaltzin and queen Xochitl, with some of their vassals, were overtaken before arriving at Tultecaxochitlalpam, which I suppose was at the hills of Tlalmanalco, and had to struggle man to man, the king perishing at the hands of his enemies, without his great age serving him as a protection, and the queen, without any respect being paid to her bravery, her sex or her beauty. This was the tragical end of a heroine worthy of being celebrated in poetry. Topiltzin took refuge in a cave at Xico, from whence he escaped after the retreat of his enemies, marching to Tlalpalan, which as I believe, was the kingdom of Aculhuacan, where he decreed certain laws which were confirmed by Netzahualcoyotl, and lived much esteemed until the day of his death.

The rest of the Toltecs were disseminated over different parts; some of them left for the coasts of the Southern Ocean and Cuauhtemalan, and others went to Tehuantepec, Coatzacoalco, Campeachy and Xacolotlan.

It was in this way that the monarchy now disappeared, which had left such fair pages in history; pages which I have compiled from Don Fernando de Alva Ixtlilxochitl.

More than an age (of 52 years) after the destruction of the Toltecs, the numerous and ferocious tribe of "Chichimecas" arrived in the valley of Mexico, who, guided by their king Xolotl had emigrated from their country, Amaquemecan, a place situated in the Northern regions of Anahuac. Huasteca, Cohuatlicamac and Tepenence bore traces of their transit, as also other points known by the name of Nopohualco or Contadero (counting-place) and these were the places where they rested some days to pass review. The king Xolotl, with the view of ascertaining the number of his people, at a given spot, ordered the number of stones to be counted, of which one had been thrown down by each individual. During their peregrination, they found the cities and towns, such as Tula and Teotihuacan, which had formerly been prosperous and flourishing, now sad, deserted and in ruins, and on their arrival at the Valley of Mexico, the Toltecs were disseminated over places afar off, such as Tehuantepec, Quauhtemalan, Teocotlan, Coatzacoalco and Tiauheohuac, and reconcentrated in a larger number in Quauhtitenco, Chapoltepec, Totoltepec, Tlazalan, Cholollan, Tepexomaco and very particulary in

Colhuacan, which formed a kingdom from whose name came that of the "Colhuis."

The Chichimecas were composed of a tribe of hunters and barbarians, principally inhabiting in caverns.

Their arms were the bow and arrow, and the ancient culverin, which drove the projectile with the greatest impetus on being blown with force. They were of a medium stature but strong; of a darkish color, with black, thick and coarse long hair, and with but little beard. They dressed themselves in the skins of animals, which although cured, still preserved the hair, and with these made their "sayos" or corslets, a kind of leather casque or helmet, and the shields for their defense. The chiefs adorned their casques with colored feathers and small pieces of silver or common metal, roughly made, as also with the parasitical plant we now call moss, but which they called *pachtli*. Lastly, various trinkets of ordinary stone girded their breasts, arms and calves. The women made use of similar skins, encircling them from their waist downwards, and covering the upper part of their person with the *huipilli* of cotton, the only texture woven by them.

The Chichimecas fared upon wild vegetables and raw game, without occupying themselves in any kind of cultivation. The sovereign wore a crown of laurel with the plumage of *Quetzalli*, in the time of peace, and of oak leaves with eagle's feathers in the time of war.

The king Xolotl knowing the Toltec civilization, dictated such prudent measures from his establishment in the Valley, that they could not fail to redound to the advantage of his people. Various chiefs, by his orders, scouted over the country in every direction, in search of the Toltecs, whom they treated with the greatest kindness and consideration: the independence of their kingdom being conceded to those of Culhuacan, without any other condition than that of paying a small tribute to the Chichimeca sovereign. These dispositions gave the desired result; with the union of the families, the Chichimecas acquired the most useful attainments in arts and commenced to abandon their barbarous customs and the habit of dwelling in caves. A part of this tribe, neglecting this civilizing element occupied a large territory to the North

West of the Valley, continuing in their savage state Westward of the Othomies.

Eight years after the foundation of Tenayuca, according to Clavijero, and an age (52 years) thereafter, according to Ixtlilxochitl, six civilized tribes arrived successively from the North, under the name of Nahuatlacas: namely the *Xuchimilcas, Chalcas, Tepanecas, Acolhuas, Tlahuicas* and *Tlaxcaltecas*, the Aztecs having separated from them at Chicomoztoc (seven caves), a site that Clavijero believes he finds to the South of Zacatecas, in the ruins we know by the name of *La Quemada*. The Xuchimilcas after exploring the circuit of the Great Lake, fixed their residence at the place which to-day bears the name of the South of the Valley, and extended their dominion (without meeting with any opposition, so feared were they by the Chichimecas), as far as Tochimilco on the Southern slope of Popocatepetl and, according to Father Duran, comprising the places known by the names of Ocuituco, Tetela Ameyalpam (Tetela del Volcan) Xamiltepec, Tlacotepec, Zacualpa, (Zacualpam Amilpas), Temoac, Tlayacapa, Totolapa, Tepuztlan, Chimalhuacan (Chimalhuacan Chalco), Ehecatzingo, Tepetlizpan, Cuitlahuac (Tlahuac) Mizquic and Colhuacan, situated, the major part, in the mountain range that unites Popocatepetl with the eminences of Ajusco.

A short time after the Xochimilcas, the Chalcas arrived, and established themselves on the South Eastern part of the lake and to the North Western slope of Popocatepetl, fixing upon Tlalmanalco, as the capital of their nation, comprising the places called Amecamecan, Tenango, Ayotzinco, Chalco, Atenco and the one now called San Martin, and arranging their boundaries pacifically with the Xuchimilcas.

The Tepanecas followed after the Chalcas, and populated the Western region of the lake between the Sierra of Guadalupe and the range of hills of Naucalpam; Atzcapotzalco being the residence of the court, and Tlacopam, now Tacuba, the principal seat of the nation, which on the dominion being afterwards divided by the nobles, was extended towards the North to Tenayuca and Tlalnepantla, and on the South to Atlacuihuayan (Tacubaya) and Coyohuacan (Coyoacan) bordering towards the Sierra, with the Othomies.

The Texcucan tribe, as numerous as that of the Xuchimilcas, arrived after the Chalcas, and were led by courageous and prudent commanders, taking up their location on the Eastern part of the lake and founding the kingdom of Acolhuacan, one of the most extensive and powerful of Anahuac, whose capital was Texcoco. The Chichimecas, connecting themselves with all the most cultivated of these tribes, rapidly abandoned their customs and even their own language, identifying themselves with them. The nobles of the Texcucan chiefs, divided among themselves the foundation of other populations, some as far as Huexotla, and erected others at Tepetlaoxtoc, Chiautla, Tlautepechpa (Tepexpam) Otompam (Otumba) and many other towns.

The Tlahuicas, on their arrival, found the shores of the lake populated, and were obliged to leave behind them the Southern mountains of the valley, in order to establish their nation at Cuauhnahuac, afterwards extending themselves to the warm and rich regions of Yautepec, Huaxtepec (Oaxtepec), Acapicthlan and Tlaquiltenanco, or in other words to all the Western part of the present State of Morelos.

Notwithstanding that the lands encompassing the grand lake, were populated, on the arrival of the Tlaxcaltecas, they were assigned the Eastern borders, where for some time they held their residence. This being a warlike tribe, very numerous and increasing rapidly, it created jealousies in the neighbouring tribes, from whence dissensions arose, which it became necessary to settle by an appeal to arms. The sanguinary battle of Poyauhtlan, which the Tlaxcaltecas sustained against the confederate tribes, was favorable to the former, but in spite of their victory, they preferred to emigrate, passing over the rugged Sierra Nevada, in search of other lands, where they might establish themselves quietly and pacifically and enjoy all the advantages of an entirely free country. Some of them proceeded to Tollanzinco and Quauhchinanco and others to Quauhquechollan, but the greater number with their chief at their head, took the road to Cholula and going round by the wide slopes of Matlalcucyatl, they halted at the town of Contla, from whence they undertook the conquest of the country occupied by Ulmecas and Xicalancas, whose principal town was *Cacaxtla*, of which some vestiges may yet be seen to the West of the sanctuary of San Miguel del Milagro.

The sanguinary struggles so tenaciously sustained and the adverse battle of Xocoyucan, obliged these tribes to emigrate, some of them taking a direction towards Zacatlan and Otlatlan to the East of their country, and others towards the plains of Apam until stopping at *Huchuechocan*, which word means to say "where the old men wept", as at this place the ancients bewailed their misfortunes.

The Tlaxcaltecas, stimulated by their warlike and enterprizing spirit, extended their dominions and founded the famous republic of Tlaxcala, governed by a senate of nobles and by the heads of the two districts in which it was divided at the beginning of their government, a division which was afterwards modified by erecting two more districts.

The Huexotzincas, alarmed at the Tlaxcaltecas on account of the preponderance they were obtaining, joined the confederation of the neighbouring States and promoted a war of extermination, but without any favorable results to them, as the Tlaxcaltecas, always victorious and aided by the Texcocanos, and in presence of the indifference of the Tepanecas, succeeded in establishing their Republic on the firmest and most solid bases, and whose capital may yet be recognized in the ruins very near to the modern Tlaxcala.

The religion of the Tlaxcaltecas was in reality monotheism under the appearance of a symbolical polytheism. Their tutelary God was the gran *Camaxtle*, whose relics were guarded by the lord of Tepectipac and to which the prisoners were sacrificed during the public feasts.

The rivalry sustained by the Tlaxcaltecas against the Mexicans was the cause of their ruin and the perdition of the other Indian nations, and principally of the Aztec or Mexican race, the last that took their seat in the Valley of Mexico and whose annals are of the greatest importance, as much from the events that preceded their establishment, as from those that followed and prepared and completed their entire ruin.

In 1196, the last and most powerful tribe, that of the Nahuatlatas, arrived at the Valley of Mexico; their country was

Aztlan (the land of herons or of whiteness) situated in the Northern regions, near Huehuetlapallan and Amequemecan, to the North of the Gulf of California. During their immigration, they halted at Chicomotzoc, separating themselves, as we have already mentioned, from the other tribes who in succession proceeded to the spacious valley of Anahuac ("surrounded by water") a name which was afterwards made extensive to the whole of the Mexican territory, from its being comprised wthin the two Oceans.

It is very probable that the cause that induced the Nahuatlatos to abandon their country was that of roaming in search of better lands and more propitious to their permanency, but with respect to the Mexicans, a circumstance is related which decided their emigration, a circumstance which may be looked upon as traditional:— Huitziton, a personage of great authority amongst the Aztecas, heard in the branches of a tree the trilling of a small bird which in its song repeated the sound "*tihui*," the literal meaning of which is "*let us go.*" Huitziton being struck at this and communicating his impressions to another personage called *Tecpaltzin*, they both induced the Aztecas to leave their country, interpreting the song as a mandate from divinity. Even to the present day there is a bird known among the Mexicans by the name of *Tihuitoehan* ("Let us go home.")

In 1160 they commenced their peregrination, and passing by a large river which historians concur in being the Colorado and which discharges itself into the Gulf of California; they advanced towards the river Gila, after remaining for some time at a place known to-day by the name of "Casas grandes," not far from the shores of that river. From thence they continued their road and again took up quarters at a place to the North West of Chihuahua, now called like the previous stopping place, "Casas grandes," and whose ruins show the vast proportions of the ancient building and fortress. Leaving behind them the wide "Sierra de la Tarahumara," they afterwards went to Hueycolhuacan, now Culiacan, Capital of the State of Sinaloa, and there remained for three years, during which time they made the statue of their God Huitzilopochtli, which was to accompany them in their expedition.

From Hueycolhuacan they passed to Chicomoztoc, where they made another halt with their God Huitzilipochtli, separating themselves from the other nations of Nahualtlatas, who continued their route. After remaining for nine years in Chicomoztoc, they again commenced their travels going towards the South, by Ameca, Cocula and Colima until reaching the region of Zacatula; from whence they passed to Malinalco, continuing their route towards the North, and arriving at Tula in 1196; there they remained for 9 years and 11 more in other places near there. From Tula they went to Zumpanco in 1216, whose governor, *Tochpanecatl* offered them a frank and liberal hospitality, to the extreme of making his son *Ilhuicatl* marry with a noble Aztec maiden called Tlapacantzin, from which matrimony the Mexican kings descended. In Zumpanco they remained seven years.

From this last place they passed to Tizayocan, a town situated at 4 leagues towards the East, and it was here that Tlapacantzin gave birth to a male child who was called Huitzilihuitl. Continuing their excursion, they passed successively to Tolpetlac and Tepeyacac, where with the consent of the king Xolotl, they established themselves, but being annoyed by the Chichimeca tribes, they retired to Chapultepec, where, according to Clavijero, they staid seventeen years, or four according to Don Fernando Ramirez. The belligerent and turbulent character of the Aztecs, who always believed in conforming their actions to divine orders, did not allow them to remain at peace during their residence in Chapultepec. Manifesting, at times, submission to the king of Culhuacan, they established themselves quietly and pacifically at the places that monarch had assigned to them, and afterwards unmasking themselves, they openly declared a war of extermination, arming themselves with missiles and darts shot from cross-bows of their invention, called *Atlaltl*. After many encounters, the last affray was so calamitous to them, that those who escaped from death or slavery found themselves obliged to seek refuge amongst the rushes of the lake. Continually persecuted by several tribes, they abandoned Chapultepec and passed to Acocolco, a group of islands situated at the Southern extremity of the lake of Texcoco. There they saw on a nopal (cactus opuntia) which sprung from the fissure of a rock, a large and beautiful eagle, with its wings extended and devouring a serpent with its talons. This event, according to their beliefs and traditions, indicated to them the spot where they ought to found their city, as in fact they did build it there, about the year 1325, giving it the name of *Tenochtitlan*, which, according to some writers, was derived from *Tenoch*, the chief of the founders; and from *Tetl*, stone, and *nochtli*, nopal, according to others; but this last interpretation has been victoriously refuted by Don Fernando Ramirez and Don Eufemio Mendoza.

During their peregrination, the tribe was divided into two factions, a dissension which produced its effect after the foundation of Mexico, by some of them establishing themselves in a sandy promontory called *Tlaltelolco*, and others in the group of islands, at a short distance therefrom.

The name of Mexico was also given to the new city, in honor of the tutelary God Huitzilopochtli, who it is believed by many to a certain degree, is the selfsame chief Huitziton deified. "The Mexican traditions (Treatise of Eufemio Mendoza) as preserved in the most ancient histories, relate that *Huitzilopochtli* was born of a virgin who belonged to the noble family of Citli (free and ancestral); that his cradle was the heart of a "maguey" plant (metl), and hence the name of *Mecitli*" afterwards changing in to *Mexitli*.

Señor Ramirez, in a valuable *historical–hierogryphical history of the peregrinations of the Aztec tribes*, which I published in my Atlas of the Republic, circumscribes the Aztec peregrination within very narrow limits, which do not extend farther than over a very small part outside of the valley of Mexico, and indicating as the point of departure, the town of Culhuacan then situated on the borders of the lake.

The ruins scattered over our territory, the historical reports and above all the distribution of the languages in accordance with those reports, cause vacillation in regard to the assertions of Señor Ramirez. Perhaps the work now being prepared by Señor Orozco y Berra may resolve the question.

The indomitable character of the Mexicans was displayed against the misdeeds of their enemies, and stimulated them to change the form of the government which until then had ruled the destinies of the nation, and had been composed of the principal members of the nobility. They resolved upon establishing their monarchy upon the surest bases of order and respectability and chose as their king Acamapitzin (1352) a descendant of Tochpanecatl and one of the most valiant and prudent of men.

This resolution at once inspired the jealousy and fears of their enemies, who moreover, being instigated by the Tlaltelolcos, the rivals of the Mexicans, oppressed the latter by their extortions and tributes, but without ever succeeding in domineering them. It was thus that this growing nation existed for 50 years, destined as it was to rule in the process of time.

The following gives the succession of its kings:

Acamapitzin.	1352 to 1389
Huitzilihuitl	1389 to 1410
Quimalpopoca.	1410 to 1422
Izcoatl	1423 to 1436
Moctezuma Ilhuicamina or Moctezuma I. .	1436 to 1464
Azayacatl.	1464 to 1477
Tizoc	1477 to 1480
Ahuitzotl	1480 to 1502
Moctezuma Xocoyotzin or Moctezuma II . .	1502 to 1520
Chitlahuatzin.	1520
Cuauhtemotzin.	1521

ETHNOGRAPHICAL PART

THERE is much to be said in regard to the indigenous race, numerous and extended as it is throughout the territory of the Mexican Republic: its habits and inveterate customs, diametrically opposed to those of the white and mixed races, influence as much in its non-increase, as they tend to the growth and invigoration of the other two.

If we make a careful examination of the state of the population in different parts of the Republic, we shall find the fact confirmed and our assertions corroborated, when stating that the indigenous race is gradually approaching towards its complete extinction.

The numerous tribes that formerly populated the fertile lands of our frontier States have completely disappeared, as may be observed in New Leon; or are found only in a very limited number, sojourning on the banks of the rivers or in the hidden depths of the mountain ranges, as happens in the States of Sonora and Chihuahua; or are intermixed with the other races in the larger towns.

The preponderance of the "Tarascos" in the ancient kingdom of Michoacan, no longer exists in that State of the Mexican Confederation. Although it be certain that a small portion of the "Tarascos," especially in the Western part of the State, still preserve their traditions and customs, the rest have incorporated themselves with the mixed race, adopting their habits and even forgetting their primitive language.

Nearly all the States of the Republic offer us a like examples. Of the traits that characterized the indigenous race, some are similar and others differ remarkably. In the craggy ravines of Tarahumara between Chihuahua, Sonora and Sinaloa, the natives exist in their natural and independent state, still preserving their ancient traditions and customs : in the central table-lands, and in general in a state of degradation, they exercise those acts of the religion that was imposed upon them by the conquest, always propending towards idolatry and a blinded fanaticism: in the mountainous districts, imbued in their ancient habits, they preserve their customs, dress and dialect, and there may be frequently found amongst them, the practice of their former religious ceremonies, simulated under the safeguard of the public manifestation of their newer faith.

Pantomimic dances are the general and most characteristic expression of their rejoicings; composed on the frontier of savage evolutions around some unfortunate victim; on the river-borders of merry and inoffensive rustic sports; in the wild mountainous regions, imitating the dances, of the *Cegador*, the *Tehuacanzi* and *Zempoalxochitl*, and again in the distant highlands of Tabasco, of pantomimes, in which the Indians dress themselves up in the old Spanish fashion.

Misconfidence, dissimulation, cunning, obstinacy and an inclination for spirituous drinks, are other general characteristics of the Indian, although he is brave, daring and long-suffering. Occasionally we see in him the dexterous hunter, climbing the heights of craggy mountains, and again we meet with him as the fearless soldier in the midst of battle, frequently after a fatiguing march of perhaps some twenty leagues or more.

Many circumstances show that the degradation of the Indian race is not derived from their original nature, but from their customs and mode of living. In a former treatise, I referred to the causes that are inimical to their natural development, which from their aptness, I shall now repeat. If we consider the Indian from the time he is born or even before his birth, we shall only find a series of lamentable wretchedness. The Indian women, even when far advanced in pregnancy, do not abstain from hard labor, and without any care for their coming offspring, continue grinding their corn; an occupation that cannot be otherwise than injurious to parturition. Then, before the proper time for taking the child from the breast, it is fed with improper nourishment and difficult of digestion; which occasions diarrhea or other infirmities that either cause its death or at the least contribute to an imperfect development.

The small-pox, owing to the carelessness, repugnance or indolence of the parents as regards vaccination, is the cause of deplorable ravages in this race, more especially among the individuals that live at any considerable distance from central populations.

The Indians are strong by nature; and it is only for this reason that it can be understood how many of them reach an advanced age, in spite of their scarce and humble food, their unhealthy mode of living, and their damp and unwholesome habitations, consisting of miserable huts, where whole families are huddled together.

Another circumstance, to which attention should be called, causes the degeneration of the Indians, and this consists in their premature marriages. In this Republic, the marriageable age for women, medically considered, has been fixed at eighteen years, and in the *tierra caliente* or hot country, at fourteen, but between this doctrine, and the actual results, so fatal to propagation, there exists an immense distance.

To these causes, which contribute so directly to the falling off of the Indian race, must be added their gradual disappearance, arising from their incorporation with other races, and the heavy decrease from losses in campaign, composing, as they do, the major part of the army.

On studying the character, habits and customs of the different tribes inhabiting the Mexican Republic, it is observed that not all of them are found in like circumstances respecting their condition, docility and civilization. Amongst some, such as the *Comanches, Apaches* and *Seris* of the Northern frontier, barbarism is met with in all its plenitude: perfidy, treachery and cruelty are the essential qualities of their character: wandering away from their hordes, they are those who principally infest our border States, destroying and killing all before them and preventing, by their depredations of every species, the development of the boundless wealth of that country. Other Indians, more or less civilized, dwell in the midst of distinct races, dedicating themselves to agricultural pursuits, to making coarse cotton cloth, baskets and mats, as well as to the manufacture of common earthenware and hats, and to the production of butter and cheese, and burning charcoal, and disposing of all these articles in the larger towns or at the fairs called "*tianguis*" or markets, that are held weekly in the villages, where they attend in large numbers, in their showy costumes.

I shall now proceed to give the distribution of the different races that inhabit the territory of the Republic, showing the numbers of which each one is composed, according to my opinion, for which purpose I have not spared in my calculations any of the means advised by prudence for obtaining, as exactly as possible, the relation which each one bears to the others. Consulting the "Geography of languages" by Señor Orozco y Berra ; the memoirs of the Government of Oaxaca, the reports from the Bishopric of San Luis, and especially those for which I am indebted to the kindness of the Curates of the States of Mexico, Morelos, and Hidalgo and the Federal District, as well as to the authorities and private individuals of other important States of the Republic, such as Michoacan, Tlaxcala, Jalisco, Aguascalientes and Sinaloa, I have been enabled to bring to a close a task which is in itself very laborious.

Like to every statistical work that is engaged in, some defects will naturally occur, which time alone can rectify.

Señor Orozco y Berra, by his "Geography of languages" laid the groundwork of the Ethnographical monument of the Republic, and Señor Pimentel by his philological comparisons and his appropriate classification, solidly constructed the edifice. Reassuming this interesting work, my only desire has been to contribute towards crowning the whole with statistical data, with my own observations and with the Indian types, in the collection of which I have now been engaged more than ten years:

SYNOPSIS of the Indian languages of Mexico, formed according to the classification of D. Francisco Pimentel.

GROUPS.	FAMILIES.	LANGUAGES.	DIALECTS.
		1st Order. — Languages polysylabic, polysynthetic of sub-flexion.	
MEXICAN-OPATA.	I. Mexican.	1. Mexican, Nahuatl or Azteca	Conchos, Sinaloense, Mazapil, Jalisciense, Ahualulco, Pipil, Niquiran.
		*2. Cuitlateco...	
		3. Opata, Teguima or Teguima Sonorense.	
		4. Eudebe, heve or hegue, dohme or dohemabatuco	
		5. Joba, joval ova	
		6. Pima, nevome, ohotama or Otama	Tecoripa. Sabaqui. Various.
		7. Tepehuan	
		8. Papago or Papabicotan	
		9 to 12. El Yuma comprising el Cuchan, el Cocomaricopa or Opa, el Mojave or Mahao, el Diegueño, or Cuñeil, el Yavipai, Yampai and yampaio	
		13. El Cajuenche, Cucapa or Jallicumuay	
		14. El Sobaipure	
		15. El Julime	
	II. Sonorense or Opata-Pima.	16. El Tarahumar	Varogio or Chinipa, Guazapare, Pachera and others.
		17. El Cahita or Sinaloa	Yaqui, Mayo Tehueco ó Zuaque.
		18. Guazave or Vacoregue	
		19. Chora, Chota, Cora del Nayarit	Muutzicat, Teacucitzin, Ateanaca.
		20. Colotlan	
		21. Tubar	Various.
		22. Huichola	
		23. Zacateco	
		24. Acaxee or Topia, comprising el Sabaibo, Tebaca, and el Xixime, the last of doubtful classification	
	III. Comanche Soshone.	25. Comanche, Nauni, Paduca, Hietan or Getan. 26. Caigua or Kioway.—27. Shoshone or Chochone.—28. Wihinasht.—29. Utah, Yutah or Yuta.—30. Pah-Utah or Payuta.—31. Chemegue or Chemehuevi.—32. Cahuillo or Cawio.—33. Kechi.—34. Netela.—35. Kizh or Kij.—36. Fernandeño.—37. Moqui and some others spoken in the United States.	Various.
	IV. Texana or Coahuilteca.	38. Texano or Coahuilteco	Various.
	V. * Keres Zuñi.	39. Keres ó Quera	Kiwomi or Kivome, Cochiteumi or Quime, Acoma and Acuco.
		40. Teauque or Tegua	Various.
		41. Taos, Piro, Suma, Picori	
		42. Jemez, Tano, Peco	
		43. Zuñi or Cibola	
	VI. Mutsun.	44. Mutsun.—45. Rumsen.—46. Achastli.—47. Soledad.—48. Costeño or Custaneo and other languages of California	
	VII. Guaicura.	49. Guaicura, Vaicura or Monqui.—50. Aripa.—51. Uchita.—52. Cora.—53. Concho or Lauretano	
	VIII. Cochimi-Laimon.	54 to 57. Cochimi, divided into four sister-languages, vizt. el Cadegomó and the languages used in the missions of San Javier, San Joaquin and Santa Maria	
		58. El Laimon or Layamon	
	IX. Seri.	59. Seri or Ceri	
		60. Guaima or Gayama	
		61. Upanguaima	

GROUPS	FAMILIES	LANGUAGES	DIALECTS
	X. Tarasca.	62. El Tarasco............ 63. El Chorotega de Nicaragua...........	
	XI. Zoque-mixe.	64. El Mixe .... 65. El Zoque............ 66. El Tapijulapa............	Various.
	XII. Totonaca.	67. El Totonaco (mixed language)............	Four
		2nd Order. — Languages polysylabic polysynthetic of juxta-position.	
	XIII. Mixteco Zapoteca.	68. El Mixteco............ 69. El Zapoteco............ 70. El Chuchon............ 71. El Popoloco............ 72. El Culcateco............ 73. El Chatino............ 74. El Papabuco............ 75. El Amuago............ 76. El Mazateco............ *77. El Solteco............ *78. El Chinanteco............	Eleven. Twelve. Two. Two. Two.
	XIV. Pirinda or Matlalzinca.	79. Pirinda or Matlalzinca............	Various.
		3rd Order. — Languages Paulosylabic Syntethic.	
Families imdependent among themselves and of the Mexican-Opata group.	XV. Maya.	80. Yucateco or Maya............ 81. Punctunc............ 82. Lacandon or Xochimel............ 83. Peten or Itzae............ 84. Chañabal, Comiteco, Jocolobal............ 85. Chol or Mopan............ 86. Chorti or Chorte............ 87. Cakchi, Caichi, Cachi or Caiqi............ 88. Ixil, Izil............ 89. Coxoh............ 90. Quiche, Utiateco............ 91. Zutubil, Zutugil, Atiteca, Zacapula............ 92. Cachiquel, Cachiquil............ 93. Tzotzil, Zotzil, Tzinanteco, Cinanteco............ 94. Tzendal, Zendal............ 95. Mame, Mem, Zaklohpakap............ 96. Poconchi, Pocoman............ 97. Atche, Atchi............ 98. Huaxteco............ *99. Haitiano, Quizqueja or Itis, with their affinities, el Cubano, Borigua and Jamaica..	Various
	XVI. Chontal.	*100. El Chontal doubtful in its morphologic character............	
	XVII. Derivatives of Nicaragua.	*101. Huave, Huaxonteca............ *102. Chiapaneco............	
	XVIII. Apache.	103. Apache............	North American Apache, Mexican Apache, Mimbreño, Pinaleño, Navajo, Xicarilla or Faraon, Lipan Mescalero.
		4th Order. — Languages cuasi-monosylabic.	
	XIX. Othomi.	104. Othomi or Hiahiu............ 105. Serrano............ 106. Mazahua............ 107. Pame............ 108. Jonaz or Meco. (Perhaps the rests of the ancient Chichimeco)............	Various

NOTE : The sign * indicates that the classification is doubtful.

I

THE MEXICAN FAMILY.

THE Mexican family, which is the most numerous, extends itself from the river of Sinaloa to the Austral or Southern regions of the Republic, and occupies a part of the State of Sinaloa, a very few portions of Durango, the Southern part of San Luis Potosí; the districts 8 and 9 and other towns of Jalisco; 7 to 8 towns of Colima; the seaboard littoral of Michoacan; the greater part of the country in the States of Guerrero, Mexico, Tlaxcala, Morelos, Puebla, the Federal District, and Veracruz, and a part of the State of Hidalgo; and is found in smaller numbers in Oaxaca, Tabasco and Chiapas. In Aguascalientes, native population is scarce, and the same occurs in the State of Chihuahua, towards the regions occupied by the Conchos and Chinarras, in regard to whose existence I have been unable to obtain any data.

In the Mexican family in particular, there may be observed the same results as in the Indian race in general: that is their decrease in the Northern regions and their greater concourse towards the South. In Sinaloa but few families have survived the former inhabitants. Jalisco has retained a larger number of them, and once in Mexico and the other more Southerly States they are still more numerous.

The Mexican race, similar to the others that populate the territory of the Republic, is extremely debased and prostrated in the vicinities of the large cities. It is here that those types of repugnance are observed, covered with rags and frequently intoxicated, carrying their loads on their backs and returning to their miserable huts, after selling their articles at a vile price.

For a better knowledge of the races, their real characteristics, their uses and customs should be studied, as I have mentioned on another occasion, in the depths of the mountainous regions where they still preserve their ancient habits and their dialects with greater purity. Tlapacoyan at the foot of the Sierra of Tezuitlan, and Amatlan in the neighbourhood of Cordoba, both in the State of Vera Cruz, display to us the best types of the Mexican family. (See the plates at the end of work.

The Indians of Tlapacoyan are engaged in agriculture and especially in the production of tobacco and coffee, which plantations compose the principal wealth of the district. The men who are less active and industrious than the women, dedicate themselves to field-labor, and are simply dressed in white drawers of "manta" (a coarse cotton cloth) and a black or coffee-colored woollen *coton* or shirt. The women who are much more cleanly than the men, use petticoats and *quichi-quimel* of white linen, a plain garment, which is converted into an elegant dress on Sundays and feast-days. On these occasions they really attract attention, on observing them parading through the towns, almost always, in company two by two, going to or coming from the churches and stores and displaying their gay attires. These are composed of a white skirt, terminating in a border of blue or red check, and of a pretty *huipilli* which descends in graceful folds, down to the knee, and which is tastefully embroidered with braiding and ribbons of various colors, that have a very showy effect. Around their necks, are hung strings of rosaries, which are nothing else but necklaces of coral or glass beads, or small silver coins, whilst their ears are ornamented by large gilt metal earrings; and lastly they wear the *mastahual*, a headdress of ribbons, above their braided and lustrous jet black hair which so well becomes their clear and olive complexions.

When external religious demostrations were allowed, the men took great pains, especially during the festivities of Corpus Christi, in ornamenting poles of a bamboo called *tarro* (giant cane), each endeavouring to excel the other in the dimensions of his bamboo, and in the beauty of its decorations. The young unmarried men attached a species of doll to the extremity of the *tarro*, in representation of their betrothed, thus making known their conquests amidst public rejoicings.

A custom which is essentially oriental, is still preserved

among these Indians. They revere and respect the moral duties of woman, so deeply, that on the occasion of their marriage, they make known whether she has preserved her purity or not, which influences in a decisive manner the esteem or contempt her person is entitled to.

In the first event, on the day after the wedding, the grand feast and ball of the *Tehuacanzi* takes place, at which the bouquet of the *zempoalxochitl* plays an important part. In the course of the feast, in front of each other they are made to dance the "ramo" and the *coconete*, which is a wax doll that is introduced intentionally for the purpose of indicating to the woman, her future destiny. The *axole* is circulated, which is a kind of *atole* or gruel made from indian corn and chocolate of which all partake, and after the warmest demonstrations of gladness, the feast concludes by the withdrawal of the bride and bridegroom; she honored and beloved and he contented and satisfied.

In the second case, the dance of the *coconete* is suspended, and on distributing the *axole*, it is presented to the bride and her father in a *jicara* or large cup perforated at the bottom, so that on taking into their hands, the liquid is spilt. The father and daughter know what this means, and both retire under the most disagreeable impressions, to hide their shame in their humble dwelling.

In Sinaloa, the virgins were accustomed to wear a mother-of-pearl shell, hanging from the neck which it was ignominious for them to lose before their marriage. This, they retained until the moment in which the husband publicly detached that ornament from their bosom, as a manifestation that they had preserved their maidenhood. This proves that the custom of the Indian women of Tlaliscoyan is very primitive.

In Amatlan, near Cordoba, the same neatness and elegance in the dress of the Indians, is observed. The labors of the "amatecos" are dedicated to agriculture, and especially to the cultivation of ananas, pine-apples and coffee, of which they possess large plantations, and it may be safely asserted that from the crops of the last few years, they have obtained a profit of more than $ 300,000. These Indians are great producers and are much inclined to trading in the Cordoba market, but, as I am assured by the merchants of that place, they have the custom of hiding away the money they receive from the sale of their produce and merchandize.

The second group of Plate III represents the types of the "Amatecos," as well as of the natives of Maltrata, which are worthy of appearing in this collection. Both places pertain to the State of Vera Cruz and are on the line of Mexican Railway.

The Mexican family, as I have before stated, is the most numerous, consisting of 1.203,270 individuals.

II

THE SONORA OR OPATA-PIMA FAMILY.

THIS family is sufficiently numerous. According to the classification of Pimentel, it comprises twenty two languages, spread over the States of Sonora, Chihuahua, Durango, Sinaloa, Jalisco and Zacatecas. The *Opatas*, the *Pimas*, the *Pápagos*, *Yumas*, *Yaquis* and *Mayos* constitute the indigenous population of Sonora. The *Coras* inhabit the mountains of Nayarit and Xalisco. The *Huicholes* are in the District of Colotlan in the same State, and finally the rests of the *Tepehuanes* and the *Acaxes* reside in Durango and Sinaloa. Very few are those that now remain of the other tribes, and some have totally disappeared.

The *Opatas* inhabit the centre and the Eastern slope of the Sierra Madre, and are composed of a civilized tribe, as friendly to the white race as they are inimical to the Apaches, against whom they are always disposed to make war. Their occupations consist in the cultivation of land and cattle breeding, and in the manufacture of hats, coarse textures and a species of baskets, the materials for which latter are obtained from the gayest plumage of the feathered tribe. They live in several of the towns where the mixed race predominates, called Opodepe, Cucurpe, Tuape, Aconchi, Babiacora, Arivechi, Santo Tomás, Bacanora and Nuri in the centre; Oposura, Guazavas, Bacadehuachi, Nacori, Mochopo and Oputo in the Sierra; Chinapa Bacoachi, Cuquiurachi and Cumpas to the North. The Opatas are able–bodied, are dexterous hunters and as fleet as the game they pursue.

An anecdote which I shall permit myself to relate, will portray in a remarkable manner, the haughty character of this race:

Persecuted by Governor Gandara with very superior forces, in consequence of an insurrection, they refused to surrender themselves, even after each one at his post had shot his last arrow. Their Captain with some few who had survived the contest, took refuge on the summit of an almost inaccessible mountain and there awaited the approach of General Gandara's emissaries who had intimated their submission: beleiving themselves humiliated at the demand for the delivery of their arms, they declared to the envoys of the General their resolution to deliver themselves up to the conqueror, without abandoning their arms. Upon General Gandara's insisting in his demands and they in their resolution, their cónduct decided him to take them prisoners by force, which they avoided by an act worthy of the ancient Spartans, in throwing themselves over the precipice, at the moment the General's troops were ascending the heights.

The *Pimas* are composed of two groups; those of the Upper and those of the Lower Pimeria. The first named inhabit the towns of Caborca, Pitiquito Oquitoa, Santa Teresa, Tubutama, Magdalena, San Ignacio, Imuris, Cocospera, Tumacacori and San Javier del Bac; the second, Comuripa, Suaqui, Tocaripa, Sayopa, Onavas and San José de Pimas. This tribe is very similar in civilization to the Opatas.

The *Pápagos* are robust and of a good stature; they are warlike and very skilful in the use of the bow and arrow. They are husbandmen, and are industrious, especially in the manufacture of tasteful baskets called *coritas*, so well woven and resistant, that water can be carried in them; they cure skins and make coarse cotton textures. They inhabit the towns of Buzani, Quitovac and Zoñi, but the greater part of them are to be found in the territory of Mesilla, now belonging to the United States. The Pápagos, like the Opatas, are enemies of the Apaches, who seldom or ever expose themselves to their terrible vengeance.

The *Yumas* have their settlements on the borders of the rives Gila and Colorado.

The *Yaquis* and *Mayos* are the principal tribes dwelling on the banks of the rivers bearing their names. The Yaqui settlements are divided between eight towns or villages called Rahun, Potan, Bicam, Huirivis, Belem, Cocori, Torim and Bacum. The settlements of the Mayos are: Macoyagui, Conicari, Camoa, Tecia, Navajoa, Cuirimpo, Santa Cruz and Masiaca. They recognize the authority of the Government of the State, but, with the consent of the latter, they are under the immediate orders of a chief of their own race.

These warlike tribes, badly advised and worthy of a better fate, have rebelled upon several occasions, sustaining disastrous struggles, which have greatly influenced in their decline. The first insurrection with which history acquaints us, occurred in 1740, and was initiated by the suggestions of a criminal escaped from prison. Their uprise did not produce the result they desired, as notwithstanding that more than 9000 Indians rose against the whites, they were completely routed, and suffered a similar fate in their second rising, which happened shortly after that same occasion. From that period, we do not again find them at war, until the year 1825, since when, with longer or shorter intervals, they have continued their incursions.

The Yaquis and Mayos like all Indians are mistrustful, tenacious and apprehensive; they have but little ambition and in general conform themselves to what suffices to attend to their most urgent necessities; they live in the cane-brakes of the meadows adjoining the rivers, rather than in towns or villages, which makes it difficult to form their census.

They are the principal field-laborers of the State and are also employed in mining and various mechanical arts and trades, for which they display considerable ability; they refine saltpetre and also manufacture coarse cotton stuffs. They

1

2

3

are strong, well-featured and of a bronze complexion. Among the women, there are several that are white and of extraordinary beauty, born of Spaniards and Indians, from which circumstance they are given the name of "coyotes" (a kind of wolf). The language of the Vaquis, as well as that of the Mayos, is composed of the dialects of the Cahita or Sinaloa tongue. These Indians, of a docile, jovial and lively character, are exceedingly partial to music and dancing, and close up their labors in the field with these entertainments. Their favorite dances are the "Venado," the "Coyote," the "Tesguin" and the "Pascola;" and the music, of which an idea is given at the end of this work, reveals the sprightly disposition of the people I refer to. I regret not being able to present the types of these races, in spite of my earnest efforts to obtain them.

The *Tarahumares*, (or foot-racers, from "huma" to run and "tala" or "tara," foot) which name bears allusion to the custom these Indians have of running at their greatest speed and driving a wooden ball before them with their foot, during their career, inhabit the mountains which, on the South Western part, form the frontiers of Chihuahua with the State of Sonora. This rugged and extensive region is divided into upper and Lower Tarahumara, the first composed of the highest part and the second of the declivities of the Sierra.

Scattered, as these Indians are, by the unevenness of the country, they live almost in a state of nature, in accordance to their former condition and customs, although subject to the Government of the State. Their hovels, disseminated through the ravines, can hardly be distinguished from above, and the existence of their miserable haunts can only be discovered by the light of their fires at night time. But very few of them present themselves in the neighbouring farms, in search of employment, but are mostly confined to their fastnesses, subsisting by hunting deer, squirrels, guanas and other animals and by the cultivation of maize, beans, pepper and potatoes of good quality. The Tarahumares are robust and of a medium size; they have very little beard and their complexion is swarthy and almost copper-colored; their hair is black, long and thick, and is worn twisted into one or two braids. Their dress consists of a kind of shirt, covering the upper part of their body and joining underneath their thighs: the women on the contrary only cover the lower part from the waist downwards, by wrapping around them a woollen cloth which descends to their feet. They also use sandals and straw hats. From the age of 17 to 40 years, the *Tarahumar* is under the imprescriptible obligation of rendering military service, and of marching with his bow and quiver well provided with arrows, wherever circumstances may require it. Amongst their civil customs, their marriages are worthy of being mentioned. When an Indian arrives at manhood, the woman chosen, with her father, establish themselves for some days in the house of the bridegroom, in order that he may thus become acquainted with the qualities of his promised spouse. If the result should be favorable, his pretensions are made in due form, and the two families, as a wedding present, hasten to construct the new habitation and to provide it with all requisites and to form a garden. The race of the *Tarahumares* was discovered by the Jesuit Juan de Fonte, and he found in them a tribe, entirely different from any others he had previously met with. The docile character of these natives contributed principally to their reduction, notwithstanding their large number, which now scarcely reaches 15,000 in both Tarahumaras, although some writers make their population ascend to 40,000. The places that were formerly inhabited by them, as well as some of those that still exist, are recognized by their termination in "chic," such as *Cusihuiriachic, Basigochic, Norogachic, Panalachic,* etc.

In the mass of the population, the Sonora or Opata – Pima family, represents 69,150 individuals, divided as follows:

Yaquis . . .	13,500	on the borders of the river of their name.
Mayos. . . .	7,000	on the margins of the river of their name.
Opatas (pure) .	5,500	Centre of the State of Sonora.
Pimas. . . .	2,500	Frontier and centre of Sonora.
Tepehuanes. .	650	Interior of the Sierra of Durango.
Pápagos . . .		To the West of Sonora, on the Upper California route.
Tarahumaras. .	15,000	"Sierra Madre," between Sonora, Chihuahua & Sinaloa.
Coras. . . .	20,000	Sierra of Nayarit, State of Jalisco.
Huichola. . .	5,000	In some of the towns of Colotlan, Jalisco.
	69.150	

All these races have gradually decreased in the process of time. Sonora, a few years since, showed us a much larger indigenous population than that which it now represents. In Sinaloa, besides the Mexican family (which is the most extensive) there exist other tribes in reduced number, such as the *Tehuecos* or *Zuaquis* between the Fuerte and Sinaloa rivers; the *Vacoregues* near the mouth of the Fuerte; the *Acaxees*, who formerly occupied the Topia Valley in Durango, in the Sierra Madre; the *Sabaibos*, the *Teobacas* in Badirahuato and the *Xiximas* at the boundary of the State with the District of San Dimas in Durango. Many other tribes have disappeared from the Sinaloa territory.

III

THE COMANCHE OR SHOSHONE FAMILY.

THE *Comanche* family considered ethnographically comprises many languages, namely: *Comanche* in the Western region of Texas and Eastern part of New Mexico: *Caigua* or *Kioway*, *Shoshone*, in the Rocky Mountains, near the heads of the Colorado and Columbia rivers; the *Wihinasht* to the West of the former; the *Pah-utah* or *Payuta* in the neighbourhood of the Great Salt Lake, the *Chemeque* or *cheme-huevi*, to the West and South of the Yutas; the *Calmillo* or *Caiwio*, the *Kechi* in the mission of San Luis Rey; the *Netela* in that of San Juan Capistrano, the *Kizh* or *kij* in that of San Gabriel, the *Fernandeño*, and finally many others spoken in the United States, to whose territory all the Comanche tribes now belong. Their devastating incursions into the Republic of Mexico are organized in Texas and New Mexico.

The Comanches have no precise idea of their origin, and only preserve a confused tradition that they came from the North; but are ignorant as to the place and period of their emigration. They also have a tradition that another race inhabited the country before them, and add that there was a time when the whole earth was covered with water, and that its inhabitants were converted into birds, in order that they might be saved from the terrible inundation. After this catastrophe, the Great Spirit created the Comanche, notwithstanding that they give themselves the name of *Na-uni* which signifies the "first living being" or "the living people."

The *Great Spirit* is for them the *Supreme Being*, although they worship other Gods, amongst which they count the Sun, the Moon and the Earth. The Great Spirit lives far beyond the Sun; his will is supreme and he dispenses good and evil, as also life and death. They tribute adoration to him, by offering up certain sacrifices, making use of fire, both in their religious ceremonies as well as in their revelries and on ministering medicines.

When the Comanches give a promise, they swear by their father the Great Spirit or by their mother, the Earth.

According to observation, these tribes do not recognize any priestly orders, nor any real system of government. Each tribe elects a military chief from amongst its bravest and most sagacious members, who is degraded immediately any act of cowardice is noted in him.

Matters of general interest are resolved in a council, which initiates the discussions by invoking some divinity. The tribes have the right of calling their separate meetings; and the chiefs of all of them, that of summoning the general assemblies.

Without subjection to any law whatever, as a consequence of their total ignorance of any form of government, each individual is the judge of his own actions and administers justice by himself, avenging the offenses he may have received. It is thus that they comprehend liberty, which they believe to proceed from the Great Spirit.

Disacknowledging the right of property, the Comanches enjoy their lands in common, so much so that the one who kills an animal, can only dispose of the skin or hide whilst others share out the meat: only prisoners of war can belong to them privately, and whom they sometimes put to death and at others exchange for the articles they require or retain them as slaves. When the captive is a child, he is considered as one of the family and is given á proper education.

As polygamy is permitted amongst them, they keep their wives as long as it suits them, even although mutual consent may be necessary to get rid of them, without which circumstance they expose themselves to the vengeance of the relations of their consorts.

Adultery by the women is punished, sometimes by death, but frequently by cutting off their noses.

Led as they are by their instincts of liberty and preferring a nomadic life, the Comanches do not trouble themselves with tilling their lands, but are engaged only in hunting or in stealing horses and mules, depredations which they commit principally in Mexican territory.

Buffalo meat is their general food. They start on their hunting expeditions on the approach of the winter, the season at which they meet in their neighbourhood with large droves that come down from the mountains. It is very seldom that they eat mule or horseflesh, as when they decide upon stealing these animals, it is generally for the purpose of exchanging them for powder, arms or other effects.

The Comanches count with their fingers, whence it results that their system of arithmetic is decimal.

As respects medicine, the knowledge they possess is very limited, and may be confined to the use of a few roots and herbs with which they heal their wounds. Singing and various superstitious practices are inherent to the application of their remedies.

Their astronomical attainments are reduced to knowing the polar star, which serves them as a guide in their travels and is called by them the "immovable star:" they are accustomed to divide time by lunar periods, but they are more commonly ruled by the change in the seasons; by cold, heat, the growth of the grass, the falling of the leaves, etc.

They believe that the earth is one immense and immovable plain, but they know very well that the cause of the eclipses is the interposition of some planet. One of the customs of the Comanches, before the grave of their relation or friend, is to sacrifice one of his horses and to burn his best chattels; and formerly they used to put his wife to death. They believe in the immortality of the soul, and maintain the illusion that the brave men or those of eminent merit, after their transit on earth, reside at a place that is paradise for them, the mansion of plump and innumerable buffaloes. At stated periods they commemorate their deceased, and on these occasions the widows scarify their arms and legs in sign of grief.

The costume of the Comanche is of coarse cloth or of buffalo hide and consists in a kind of loose jacket ("sayo") and trowsers or leggings sometimes adorned with pieces of silver. They paint their faces with different colors and ornament their hair profusely. In their fights, they present themselves almost in a state of nudity.

The Comanches are in general very robust and tall, good horsemen and proverbial for their skill in the use of their arms which consist principally in the bow and arrow.

They have no regard for females and only consider them necessary for domestic labor, notwithstanding the participation they concede them in all the acts of their errant and warlike life. After an affray, it is they who commit the greatest acts of cruelty, martyrizing the prisoners for the space of three days, after which they kill them. The Comanches eat the flesh of their prisoners, not so much as food, as to assuage their repugnant spirit of revenge. Notwithstanding, it is said that these savages are hospitable with friendly foreigners.

IV

THE TEXANO OR COAHUILTECA FAMILY.

MR. Pimentel has denominated as the *Texian* or *Coahuilteco* language that which was formerly the most used in Coahuila and Texas and was spoken from Candela to the river of San Antonio. These tribes were known by the names, of *Pajaletes, Orejones, Pacaos, Pacoas, Jilijayos, Alasapas, Pansanes, Pacuaches, Mescales, Pampopas, Tacames, Chayopines*

Venados, Pamaques, Pihuinques, Borrados, Sanipaos and *Manos de perro* (dog's paws.)

The frontier States and very particularly, Coahuila, New Leon and Tamaulipas, present us the evident proof of the gradual disappearance of the indigenous race.

In the New Leon territory, there existed several wandering tribes without any political organization, who were only subject to the obedience of a Chief and lived on game and wild fruit.

Of the tribes whose names are hereafter expressed and who have disappeared, some have been classified by Mess[rs] Orozco y Berra and Pimentel, and others have not received any classification on account of their languages having been lost.

The South of New Leon was inhabited by the *Pames* (*Othomi* family) *Janambres, Pasitas* and *Aliguanes.*

In the lands of Linares, the *Cademas, Hualahuises,* and *Come-pescados* (fish eaters.)

In those of Monte Morelos and Teran, the *Borrados* and *Rayados.*

In those of Monterey, the *Huachichiles, Aguaceros* and *Malinceños.* In Salinas and Marin the *Cuanales* and *Aiguales.*

In Vallecillo, the *Ayaguas* and *Garzas.*

In Lampazos and Agualeguas, the Indians of the *Malnombre* and *Tobosos* tribes, who came from Coahuila and inhabited the Northern part of this State, and pertained to the Apache family.

In Bustamante, the *Alzapas* and *Coahuiltecos.*

At the period of the conquest of New Leon by Carbajal, the whole of the tribes of that territory counted upon a population of 35,000 individuals. The thraldom to which they found themselves reduced, compelled them to rise and maintain a war of casts which lasted two hundred years. The losses incurred in so prolonged a struggle, their emigration to distant parts and their indifference as to the preservation of their race and language, caused their ruin to such an extent, that not one of these natives exists in this State of the Mexican Confederation.

The numerous ruins of ancient edifices now to be found in the State of Tamaulipas, indicate the existence of other inhabitants long before the conquest, and show that they were not in the same state of barbarism, as was met with at that period. The ruins of the valley of Santa Barbara and those that exist in the "cañadas" of the Sierra, prove an antiquity and civilization much greater than that of the former populations of Altamira. According to Orozco y Berra, the remains that are still to be found at Santa Barbara, may be traced to the civilized nations that perished at the time of the irruption of the "Chichimecas."

The *Huastecas* who separated themselves from the Toltecs and intermingled with the *Nahoan* nation, which inhabited a part of Tamaulipas, established themselves from the river Tuxpam up to the borders of the Panuco. At the present, bu very few of this indigenous race remain in Tamaulipas.

V

THE KERES ZUÑI FAMILY.

ACCORDING to Pike, the *Keres* Indians form the principal part of the indigenous population of New Mexico, and are distinguished in their physical nature for their tall stature, and in their moral qualities for the mildness of their character: they live isolated from the whites, still preserving their former habits and dedicating themselves to agricultural labors in the towns of Santo Domingo, San Felipe, Laguna Acoma, Santa Ana Silla and Cochiti.

The *Tesuques* or *Teguas* belong to this family and inhabit the towns of San Juan, San Ildefonso, Nambre, Santa Clara Pojuaque and Tesuque. The *Taos*, residents of the places called Taos, Picori, Sandia and Isleta: the *Jemez* of the place of the same name and the inhabitants of Zuñi, numbering altogether 2,000 persons, also belong to it.

The capital of the Zuñis was the famous city of Cíbola,

which figures so much in the narrations of the first explorers of New Mexico, and which appeared to Father Niza even more considerable than Mexico, and the finest and most important city of all those then discovered. Father Zarate, like many others, did not participate in the admiration of the former missionary respecting the grandeur of Cibola, as he states simply that "Juan de Oñate arrived at the province of "Zuñi, where the country was more thickly populated with "hares and rabbits than with Indians: there are six towns, "in the whole of which there are not over three hundred hou- "ses of several stories like those of New Mexico: the largest "town and the head of the others is Cibola, which in their "language they call Ha-huico; it has one hundred and ten "houses: the food like that of these parts in general, consists "of maize, beans, pumpkins and game: the people dress them- "selves in cloth made from the fibres *(pita)* of the agave, as "they have no cotton." The same exaggeration regarding the grandeur of Cibola, occurs with Quivira, as appears in his different writings.

This is the information, respecting this family, which I have taken from Mr. Pimentel's work ("Cuadro descriptivo y comparativo de las lenguas indigenas de México"), in which will be found many other details that I omit, for the reason that they treat of an ethnographic family, not pertaining to Mexican territory.

VI

MUTSUN FAMILY.

THE Indians of this family inhabit Upper California, and their number has decreased to so gradual and considerable a degree that it is believed that the race has disappeared.

Belonging to the *Mutsun* family, are the *Rumsens*, *Achastlis*, the Indians of *La Soledad*, the *Costeños* and others composing the tribes of California.

In accordance with the purpose I have proposed in treating of the indigenous tribes that inhabit the Mexican territory, I have made only a slight indication as to those who dwell in the United States, so as not to vary from the order of classification made by Mr. Pimentel.

VII & VIII

GUAICURA AND COCHIMI-LAIMON FAMILIES IN LOWER CALIFORNIA.

THE native Indians of Lower California, whose number in the earlier years of the conquest was estimated at more than 20,000 have followed the lot reserved by destiny to all the race in general. The principal populators were the *Cochimis* in the Northern districts; the *Guaicuras* in the centre, and the *Pericues* in the Southern extremity of the Peninsula. Of these three nations the *Pericues* were the most indomitable and those that disappeared the first; the other two sharing the same fate, some time afterwards, being gradually annihilated by the profound grief with which they were filled at finding themselves obliged by the missionaries to abandon their ancient creeds, their customs and even their own language.

According as the indigenous race has continued dissappearing from the Californian soil, it has been successively superseded by another population, generally of a mixed race proceeding from the immigration that has taken place especially from Sonora, Sinaloa and Jalisco.

The population of Lower California now consists of 22,000 inhabitants, including in this number 2,500 wandering Indians, scattered over the North Eastern part of the Peninsula between the cordillera and the river Colorado.

IX

SERI FAMILY

THE *Seri* family, according to the classification of its dialects, includes the *Guaymas* and the *Upanguaymas*. .

The *Seris*, savage Indians of ferocious instincts and much addicted to the vice of drunkenness, are met with in a very reduced number in the Island of Tiburon and the adjacent coasts of Sonora. They support themselves by fishery and by stealing cattle; they use poisoned arrows which cause immediate death, however slight many be the wound, and are always at war with the white race.

Formerly there was a numerous tribe which extended itself from the coasts of Guaymas to the river Altar, and from the same coasts to San Miguel de Orcasitas, San José de Pimas and Suaqui towards the interior. In the last century the troops garrisoned at Altar and Orcasitas, after a tenacious persecution undertaken against the Seris, succeeded with some of them in establishing the towns of Populo and Seris, near to Hermosillo, and in pacificating the rest of the tribe; but this peace was ephemeral and of but short duration, as they again rose, destroying "haciendas" and "ranchos" and have since continued being the dread of travellers, especially in the route from Hermosillo of Guaymas,

Fortunately for humanity, their number has been much reduced and barely consists of some two hundred, of more than two thousand that existed towards the end of last year.

X

THE TARASCA FAMILY.

THE rich and extensive territory of Michoacan, which now constitutes an integral part of the Mexican Confederation, previously formed the kingdom of the *Tarascos*, whose boundaries on the North were the independent tribes of the Aztec Empire, on the East this same empire, and on the West and South the great Pacific Ocean. Its inhabitants who were immigrants from the Northern regions, according to their own indications, founded their capital on the borders of lake Patzcuaro, calling it *Tzintzuntzan*, (which signifies home of the "colibri" or humming bird, derived from *tzuntzun* in imitation of the buzzing sound produced by these diminutive birds.) From the plumage of the "colibris" which are so abundant in these parts, the former inhabitants of Michoacan made elegant pictures, which formed one of their most important branches of art and still continues with their descendants. The language of the Tarascos is rich and harmonious although less abundant than Mexican in its terminations and derivatives. The Tarasca nation, of an indomitable character and very numerous, was never subject to the Aztec empire, with which by its civilization it possessed some points of contact, having acquired a knowledge of the use of hieroglyphics.

Its religion like that of the Aztecs, permitted the custom of sacrifices, but dissented in the form, its theogony not admitting the mythological complication of the Mexicans, as by all preference they rendered acts of devotion to an idol whose temple, besides that of the High Priest, was located at the summit of a high mountain of the environs *Tzacapu*. The Tarascos lived in towns and cities subject to the observance of certain laws that guaranteed individual security and which were framed under the form of an absolute government. The sovereign designated his successor. According to the very interesting and curious work lately brought to light in Spain, whose narratives were extracted from the original old manuscripts that exist in the library of the Escorial and were printed in a very limited number: the sovereign* was the representative of the God *Curicaberis*, and consequently his mandates were considered as emanating from that God. The kingdom erected into a seigniory until the arrival of the Spaniards, was divided into four parts or provinces under the immediate command of their respective caciques, who combined with their people to undertake the wars of conquest. Various chiefs accompanied the Cazonci as also the sub-delegates who filled different offices, the *Ocambecha* collected the tributes of the rich and the *pirovaque vendari* those of the poor, consisting in cotton and domestics, the *tareta vaxatati* had charge of the crops belonging to the crown with other inferior sub-delegates: the *cacari* was the superintendent of the quarries and stone-cutters; the *guavicoti* was the head gamekeeper for quadrupeds and the *curuhapindi* for birds, the game being sometimes intended for sacrifices in honor of the Goddess *Xaratanga* and at others for the table of the *Caconci:* the *varuri* was the chief of the fishermen with a net, and the *tarama* the head of the fishermen with hook and line; the *cavaspati* was the head harvestman and another officer received and stored the cane-juice and honey. The *atari* was the head butler who received all the wine made from the "maguey" (agave); the *cuzari* was the master fellmonger and manufacturer of the leather garments for the *cazonci;* the

---

* The name of the grand Caltzontzin was generally given to the king Sinziccha, the last sovereign of Michoacan, inhumanly sacrificed by Nuño de Guzman.

usguaricuri was the principal feather-maker, who worked with others of his class the ornaments made with the red plumes of the "guacamayo" (psittacus macao) and the white feathers of the heron and other birds. The *Pucuriguari* was the chief woodsman and furnisher of timber and firewood ; the *Curinguri* was encharged with making the drums and kettle-drums ; the carpenters also had their master. The Treasurer-general had in his safe-keeping the silver, gold and jewelry composed of ear-rings and bracelets of silver, and mitres and garlands or wreaths of gold ; the *Cherequegari* was the guardian of the bows and arrows; there was a master-maker of bucklers or shields of rich feathers of birds, and a storekeeper who had charge of the extensive granaries of the *Cazonci*. The *hicharutavandari* built the canoes and the *paricuti* supplied them with rowers. The war spies were commanded by a chief. The *Vazanoti* was the head of the couriers and messengers and, in the time of war, of the banners composed of magnificent plumes of feathers ; a sub-delegate had charge of the eagles and other birds confined in cages, and several men took care of the wild beasts; lastly there were many other officers, such as the head of the medical staff of the Cazonci, and masters of the painters, potters, earthenware-makers, sweepers, flower-makers and shop-keepers.

If we were obliged to judge of the civilization of the Tarascos by their inhuman acts, during their religious feasts, it would be necessary to acknowledge that it was in a barbarous state. Fantastic and even grotesque dances preceded the human sacrifices ; the priests pointing out beforehand the slaves who had to be offered up and more particularly in the principal feast called *Secuindiro*. They drew out the hearts of their victims and cast them still reeking into the thermal waters of *Araro*, doing the same with their blood in the other fountains of the place referred to, all in honor of the Goddess *Cueravaperi*, who was considered as the mother of all the Gods of the earth. Two priests called *hauripicipecha*, cut off the hair of the men and women and threw it into the fire, saturated in the blood of the sufferers. On the day after the feast, and some of them wearing the skins of those that had been sacrificed, they took part in the dances and gave themselves over to inebriety; these abominable acts lasting for five days consecutively.

In the narratives which I have extracted, mention is made of the town af *Cinapécnaro* and not of *Tzacapu*, according to some historians, as the place where the *Cue* or temple of their principal idol was erected on the summit of some eminence. In each *cue* or temple, there was a high priest, who was called the *curate* or *grand-father*, who exercised supremacy over the others and was distinguished from them by a gourd adorned with turquoises worn on the head, similar to a mitre, as well as by other ornaments, accompanied by a flint spear which they used as a kind of symbol. The other priests carried a gourd over the shoulders and discharged various duties in a manner analagous to what we have observed in civil affairs: those called *tiniccha* carried their Gods on their backs when they went to war; the *axaniccha* were the executioners, the *pasariecha* the keepers of the Gods, the *opitiecha* those who held the feet and hands of the victims who were about to be sacrificed, and the *quiquiccha* those who dragged the captives and slaves to the place of execution. Lastly the priests held their services and preached in the temples and presided over the drummers, the musicians and the common criers.

In the time of warfare, their plagaries asking for the triumph of their arms preceded their ceremonies. When war was declared against any unfriendly nation, the caciques commenced preparations immediately with all their people, placing themselves under the direct command of a Captain general whom they called the *Cazonci*. This general presented himself, richly accoutred with his plume of green feathers, a large silver shield slung over his shoulders, a quiver of tiger's skin, a doublet of scarlet cotton, ear-rings and bracelets of gold and "calzones" or leggings of tiger skin. The priests, as I have already stated, carried their Gods on their backs, and especially the God *Curicaberi* and the Goddess *Xaratanga*, in whose names the Captain general harangued his warriors.

When the legions were on the march, the people living on the route they passed by, came to meet them with provisions and cheered them enthusiastically to battle, which was nearly always for the purpose of conquest. When once the field of action was decided upon, according to the indications of the spies, and the combat was commenced, there might be seen among the armed masses, more than three hundred standards of white heron's feathers, glittering in the rays of the sun, as well as the magnificent plumes of the warriors composed also of heron and eagle's feathers or the red plumage of the "guacamaya."

Generally speaking, the Mexican frontiers were the points selected for their assaults and where the Othomies, troops in the service of Mexico, received their first onsets.—They laid ambuscades, made false retreats and feigned repulses, in order to attract the enemy to a suitable spot and fall upon him in mass at a given signal, whether this were a column of smoke or a sound from the bugle. In this way they succeeded in annihilating the enemy's forces and in capturing the greatest number of prisoners, who were afterwards sacrificed, the young boys being condemned to field labor. Their victories were signalized by massacre and incendiarism. The Tarascos held it as a high honor to die in battle, so much so that the *Cazonci* distributed recompenses to their widows and orphans, and gave symptoms of his deep sorrow.

Justice was administered in the name of the *Cazonci* and penalties were enforced according to the gravity of the crimes committed. Adulterers and thieves were sentenced to death and a like punishment was inflicted upon any one appropriating one of the *Cazonci's* women, this penalty being made extensive to the family and relations of the delinquent, as concealers of the crime; sorcerers had their mouths cut to pieces with knives and were trailed alive and stoned to death. Any serious fault of a cacique or other officer was punished by death from blows on the neck given with a club, his body being afterwards buried or given over to the voracity of the birds of prey. Habitual drunkenness of the son or brother of the *Cazonci* was expiated by death, the tutors or governesses of the delinquents being subject to a similar penalty which in certain cases was proportioned to the fault by imprisonment for a few days, by banishment, by prohibition from wearing the insignias af a warrior or by stripping the consort.

In their marriages the Tarascos performed various ceremonies, according to the rank of the contracting parties. At the matrimony of the daughter of the sovereign, a *curitiecha* priest officiated, assisted by other dignitaries. Many women accompanied the princess, dressed out and adorned with ear-rings and necklaces, and carrying the jewels, baskets and trunks. The priest made the presentation of the bride, saying to the bridegroom, "*here is the lady sent to you by the king : I bring her to you; do not quarrel; be good spouses ; bathe one another*" and he then exhorted the princess in the following words : "*thou must give to eat to this man and make him his clothing and do not quarrel : be good spouses, and if any one should enter into your house give him clothing ; the king says that whatever you may give, he gives to you.*" Other exhortations followed which were answered by the parties, conforming thereto.

In the matrimonies of the grandees and nobles, a messenger sent by the father of the wooer demanded the daughter of any noble in marriage, who after many compliments and previously consulting the case with his wives, * gave his consent, manifesting the greatest amiability. To the request for marriage, followed the preparations for the wedding, by dressing the maiden, packing the household goods and chattels, collecting the cloth for the shirts of the husband and preparing the hatchets for cutting the timber designed for the *Cues*. Matters being thus arranged, the bride departed in company with her relations and by the other women, bearers of the jewels trunks and cotton, and on arriving at the house of the bridegroom, which was already prepared for her reception with the best of entertainment, the priest presented himself, saying "*This maiden is sent to you by such a person and is his daughter : May the Gods grant that you speak the truth in asking for her and that you may be good spouses and that you render her benefits*" and then addressing himself to the woman, he spoke to her in these terms : *See that thou art not found on the road speaking with any man, and that they seize thee and that then we give cause to be ill-spoken of in our homes ; be what thou oughtest to be, as I have come to show thee the home that thou wilt have here and the habitation thou hast to form.*"

* This phrase shows that polygamy was permitted among the Tarascos.

Lastly he exhorted the man as follows: and thou, Sir, if thou shouldst note any act of adultery in thy wife, leave her quietly and send her to her house, without doing her harm, and without throwing the blame on any one but herself if she should be bad: this is so, May the Gods grant that thou mayst have understood me. The priests admonitions to the betrothed continued and the ceremony concluded with the banquet that had been prepared.

The plebeians arranged their marriages through the intervention of their families and not that of the priests. The father of the maiden counselled his daughter, saying to her: "*Daughter, thou must not leave thy husband lying down at night, whilst thou goest elsewhere to commit adultery: see that thou art not bad, that thou dost not inflict this evil upon me, that if thou art a bad omen thou wilt not live long: perhaps thy husband may enter the "cue" at vespers and thou alone seeketh thy death: remember that I did not do this; that I am thy father; that thou wilt make me shed tears, entangling me in thy corruptness, and not only will they kill thee but me also with thee:*"

Others married without the interference of their parents and some were united in fulfilment of the mutual promise of their families. Relations married with each other and repudiation was made a custom when the woman did not comply with her obligations or committed adultery.

The foregoing lines serve to show that the Tarasca nation by its civil and political institutions, constituted a really civilized people, whilst it equally deserved the title of barbarous by its religious practices.

To-day the descendants of this numerous people pay their tribute like other races to the inflexible law of destiny. As it is intermingled and incorporated in populated places with the mixed race, it decreases remarkably, forgetting its traditions, its customs and its language; and it is only in the Western part of Michoacan and in some places in the centre and the South, that they preserve their primitive customs.

The types I present in Plate IV, group 2 nd. belong to the *Chilchota* people to the South East of Zamora, a place where the Indians retain their customs in all their purity. The dress

of these Indians is composed of a woollen cassock called a gabardine, wide trowsers or "calzoneras" of cloth and leather, a woollen *zarape* or cloak called *quixchan*, leather shoes with folds, lined with green or red morocco and a straw hat. The rich women wear cloth skirts and the poor people a coarse texture woven by themselves; they use a shirt of white linen and a striped mantle or shawl, sometimes of different colors. Their trinkets consist of ear-rings of common metal or of gold or silver and coral or bead necklaces, with ribbons of colored worsted with which they adorn their hair and embroider their petticoats very prettily, and the *quichquemel*. When they marry they give the husband, as a wedding present, a waistband exceedingly well made and a napkin.

The present Tarascos have not lost the spirit of their predecessors, as they are proving daily in their contests in Michoacan, where the revolutions that now agitate that State would exist with difficulty without their help. More than fifty individuals at once have been seen to march to the place of execution and meet their death valiantly, solely for not betraying a delinquent.

The Tarascos, like all the Indian race in this particular, are extraordinarily fond of music, and the numerous orchestras they invent attract attention, formed as they sometimes are of guitars of all dimensions and even ill constructed, but from whose sounds a really remarkable harmony is produced, as also from other instruments similar to clarinets with which a like effect is produced.

The Tarascos are extended all over the State of Michoacan, in the Southern part of Guanajuato, in the valley of Mazamitla in Jalisco and in some places in Guerrero, and their number may well be estimated with very slight difference in 200,000 individuals.

XI

THE ZOQUE-MIXE FAMILY.

THE *Zoques* Indians inhabit the Western part of Chiapas, to the North of the Sierra Madre, a small portion of the South of Tabasco and the mountainous district where the towns of Chimalapa are situated in the State of Oaxaca, and the Isthmus of Tehuantepec. Formerly they occupied a small tract of land on the borders of the territory of Tabasco, forming an independent nation and well populated, which was subjugated by Marin, during his expedition to Chiapas. Their capital was called *Ohcahuay* and in Mexican *Tecpantlan* which signifies "the seat of palaces." The remains of the habitations of the former *Zoques* are still to be met with both in Oaxaca and Chiapas.

Those who reside in the districts referred to and in some parts of Chiapas, principally in the towns of Tuxtla Gutierrez and Tapijulapa are of an athletic form and are easily distinguished by the rare custom of shaving their heads all excepting on the front part. (See group 3rd. Plate IV.) As the generality of these Indians are of a docile character, but addicted to spirituous drinks, they are employed in agricultural labor, particularly in the cultivation of maize, tobacco and delicious oranges; their manufactures consisting of articles made from "pita" (the filaments of the agave) and ixtle and are much esteemed. The *Mixes* are found in the Eastern part of the State of Oaxaca where the range of mountains known as the "Sierra de los Mixes," rises between the districts of Yautepec, Tlacolula, Villa Alta and Tehuantepec, Quetzaltepec and Atitlan.

They formerly composed a numerous tribe, but are now extremely reduced. These natives, as I have already had occasion to mention, embraced christianity, but without abandonig their former creeds. They are superstitious and secretly exercise some ancient religious practices, by sacrificing birds and other animals to some of their deities.

The *Mixes* like the *Zoques* are addicted to fermented liquors and occupy themselves by preference in the labors of the fields, cultivating in their rich lands, watered by the streams of the Coatzacoalcos, maize, beans, rice and plantains. They are strong, courageous and warlike, qualities that characterized their ancestors, who were never conquered by the Mexicans and Zapotecas, notwithstanding the numerical superiority of these two nations. Their ferocious instincts and their inclination to eat human flesh and to encourage rebellion for this purpose, have disappeared, even although their actual civilization and morality leave much to be wished for.

The *zoque-mixe* family numbers 47,600 individuals, namely 21,600 zoques and 26,000 Mixes.

XII

THE TOTONACA FAMILY.

THE *Totonacas* extended from the Sierra of Huachinango, North of the State of Puebla to the Gulf coast, comprising a zone of the State of Vera Cruz between the river of Chachalacas and that of Cazones and limited by the country of the Huastecos, on the North.

According to Torquemada, the Totonacos arrived at Anáhuac before the Chichimecas, coming from the same direction, (the North) divided into twenty bands or families. The first place where they were established was at Teotihuacan, and there, according to their statement, they constructed two famous temples dedicated to the Sun and the Moon, the ruins of which still exist; but according to other accounts, these were not their work but that of the Olmecas, and were afterwards rebuilt by the Toltecas. From Teotihuacan they passed to Tenamitic and from thence to the places where they still remain. The capital of the Totonacos was Mixquihuacan, and they had besides, many well populated cities, such as Cempoala on the Gulf coast, the first that was trodden by the Spaniards:

They were governed by kings whose names were
Umeacatl.
Xatonton.
Tenitztli.
Panin.
Nahuacatl.
Ithualtzintecuhtli.
Tlaixchuatenitztli.
Catoxcan.
Nahuacatl and Ixcahauitl.

The first of these kings was the one that the Totonacos brought as their chief from the Northern countries and who reigned in peace, but during his period a terrible famine and plague came and destroyed the greater part of the population.

In the time of the second king, the Chichimecas arrived and established themselves at Nepecalco, six leagues from the Totonaco capital.

During the other three reigns, the greatest peace was preserved and nothing remarkable occurred; but Ithualtzintecuhtli had a war with those of Tecpanquimichtlan, in which he was the conqueror and left his enemies severely chastised.

The 7th and 8th kings governed in peace, the latter leaving the kingdom divided between his two sons Nahuactl and Ixcahuitl, who shortly afterwards quarrelled and the people being severed in bands, a struggle commenced, which resulted in the kings absenting themselves. Observing this, the Chichimecas charged down upon the Totonacos, and the latter being conquered were placed under the command of a chief of the other nation called Xihuitlpopoca, who was succeeded by Motecuhzuma and Quauhtlaebana.

Later on the province of the Totonacos was conquered by the Mexicans, whose tributaries they had been on the arrival of the Spaniards, which circumstance caused the first named to unite with Cortés in making war against Moctezuma."

As regards religion adds Pimentel, it appears that they adopted that of the Mexicans with its horrible human sacrifices : every three years they immolated three children whose blood mixed with a certain gum, they preserved as something sacred. Notwithstanding, in a high mountain there was a celebrated temple dedicated to the Goddess of harvests, who as we have said, did not require sacrifices of men but of animals. It is remarkable, according to Torquemada that the Totonacos practised circumcision.

The etymology of the word *Totonaca* adopted by Buschman, in his work " The names of Aztec places," is not exact, as this author adopted it as stated by D. Francisco Dominguez, saying "Totonaca signifies to the letter three hearts in one sense and three beehives in another," as *toto* means three and *naca* heart. Notwithstanding, this literal traslation does not define the meaning the word should express, which has evidently been take in a metaphorical sense. It is a fact that the number three appears to have had something mysterious about it among the Totonacos, as they not only applied it to their language, but also as we have seen, every three years they made a solemn sacrifice of three children.

In my excursion to the Sierra of Huauchinango, I had an opportunity of observing the habits and customs of the actual Totonacos, which I make known in the following lines :

The Huauchinangos are of medium stature, strong and well formed ; their hair is long, black and glossy and their complexion dark. Their appearance, looking at the profile of the face, is distinguished from that of the other natives known in the country, as much as it assimilates with that of the inhabitants of some of the Asiatic regions(With respect to their costume, all the Huauchinangos dress exactly alike, using white and wide trowsers folded nearly up to the knees, a blue woollen "coton" or shirt, a handkerchief used as a cravat and a hat made from the palm-leaf. Simple and moral in their customs, if they know any vice it is only that of intoxication.

The Totonacos, of a better and more docile character than the Mexicans, from Xico and beyond there, are of a yellower complexion, which in my opinion proceeds from the elevated temperature in which they live as well as from the humidity of the soil and their proximity to the coasts. Their dress differs from that of the Huauchinangos in the tunic, the stuff of which is of a coffee-colored and white linen.

The native women are extraordinarily clean in their persons and dress, the style of the latter being sometimes elegant. A narrow skirt called *chincue* and a *quichmequel* tastefully embroidered compose their attire. Their headdress is no less attractive; they tie their long and jet-black hair with colored ribbons and bind their heads with their well-plaited braids. (See Plate V. group 2nd.)

All those deceive themselves who pretend to know the indigenous race by the forbidding types that are seen in the large cities and their vicinities: the importance of this race, their real character, their habits and customs should be studied in the depths of the sierra, where people exist who are susceptible of the highest grade of civilization and where also may be known those who are incapable of acquiring it. The sierra of Huauchinango and the high sierra of Zacualtipan display to us, people of a distinct race and diversity of character: the one distrustful but docile and the other equally distrustful but moreover perfidious. In such a limited space of country two people are found of instincts and characters diametrically opposed to each other; qualities that are found even in their respective languages, the one being sweet and harmonious and the other harsh and guttural: such are the Mexican and the Otomi of which I shall treat towards the end of this part of my work.

The Huauchinangos are engaged in agriculture, in the fisheries and in raising cattle: they cultivate sugar cane on the slopes of the mountains and make brown sugar and "aguardiente." (rum of the country.)

It frequently happens that the traveller finds himself surprised, in the midst of his repose, by the natives who come to felicitate him, playing on their harps and other instruments, and accompanying the music with characteristic songs or executing pantomimic dances. The music, at times languid and sad and at others lively and inspiring, excites and charms the attention. They execute their dances gracefully and skilfully, the most curious and remarkable of all, known by the name of the *cegador*, is performed by men. The master of ceremonies carries a sprig of "ojite" in his hand, larger than that of the others, with which he indicates the figures that are to be successively executed by the dancers, who are arranged with symmetry, and at the first signal the dance commences, now composed of complicated pieces in which time is kept with the feet and again imitating the evolutions of the *cegador*, and lastly at a given sign from the director, they change attitudes and on meeting, touch each other with the shoulder, for the purpose of giving the body a revolving movement, which obliges them, with a certain grace, to vary their position. The dance concludes at last by executing the same figure that is observed at the termination of quadrilles, but in a more graceful way, as they never fail to keep step with the music or to imitate the movements of the *cegador*. In some places on performing these evolutions they entwine ribbons of different colors, which each one carries in his hand and this gives a very pretty effect.

In their public feasts, in their simulachres of battles, in their games and even in their religious acts, these Indians preserve their ancient traditions, but the inveterate diffidence towards civilized persons, causes a certain reserve and fear in them.

Such, in compendium, are the principal distinctive characteristics of these people who inhabit the most beautiful part of the Republic.

According to my calculation, the number of the Totonacos reaches 85,000 individuals distributed over the States of Vera Cruz and Puebla.

XIII

MIXTECO-ZAPOTECO FAMILY.

This family is composed of the individuals who speak the following languages, the last two of doubtful classification; *Mixteco, Zapoteco, Chuchon, Popolaco, Cuitlateco, Chatino, Papabuco, Amusgo, Mazateco, Solteco* and *Chianteco*.

The *Mixtecos* occupy a large extent of land, situated on the maritime littoral of the Grand Pacific Ocean, stretching itself towards the interior of the country and embracing a great part of the State of Oaxaca, a fraction of the State of Puebla and the Eastern portion of the State of Guerrero. It is divided into two regions known by the names of the Upper and Lower Mixteca. The first is composed of the mountainous range and the second of the plains adjoining the coast. According to the chronicles of the Mixteca nation, the place they proceeded from is unknown, it being simply ascertained that on their immigration by the Panuco river, they went to Tula and that having found this part well populated, they continued on to Cholula, where they were perfectly well received by the natives who related themselves to them; their first Captain being a Mixteco. After a long residence at this place, they commenced populating the broken territory of the Mixteca, whose asperities presented a natural barrier for their defense against their enemies or persecutors, as is inferred from the account of Father Burgoa. To the asperities of the soil they owed, in a great part, their victories over the Mexicans sent against them by Moctezuma. It is stated that Tilantongo was the Court of the king of the Mixtecos and that near to this frontier town, in Achutla, which is towards the West, there was a temple raised to their first Deity, to which many pilgrims came from very distant parts.

Another sanctuary, the residence of the high priest, existed in Yanhuitlan, and it was here that aged persons and women came to pray and make their offerings, who from fatigue and debility or from coming from far-off lands, were not able to scale the sharp ascents of Achutla.

The Mixtecos, in their historical annals, traced their lineage and descent by means of hieroglyphic paintings and characters on the bark of trees and on prepared skins, and it is asserted that in these inscriptions they chronicled the deluge of the world and the genealogy and biography of their forefathers and of the patriarchs. The perfect age adopted was 52 years, as in the Toltec century, that period being divided into other four of 13 years each, which they made to correspond respectively to the four cardenal points, attributing a prosperous time to some seasons and a disastrous one to others.

The period pertaining to the East was fertile and healthy; that to the North, variable: backward for the harvests, but propitious for the generation and increase of the population, that of the West; and lastly adverse and the origin of all evils, that of the South. Their year commenced approximately about the Spring equinox and consisted of 18 months of 20 days, and another month more of 5 days, which was made 6 every four years, and which was called "*menguado*" (diminished).

The Mixtecos, who were almost naked, did not use any thing more than an apron, not to offend delicacy, and more sociable than the *chontales*, they joined together in clans under the immediate command of four caciques, distributed over the districts pointed out by the four cardinal points.

The whole number of the Mixtecos reaches 220,000.

The origin of the arrogant *Zapoteca* nation has remained enveloped in obscurity. History has simply gathered some data relating to the former members of this family, whose timbres of grandeur were ciphered in their antiguity, in their warlike instincts and in their strengh of spirit, believing that they proceeded from lions and other wild beasts, from lofty trees or from immense rocks, as appeared from their pictures.

As the Emperor Moctezuma was desirous of extending the dominions of his vast empire, still more, he undertook the conquest of the Mixteco nation, with the view of leading to that of the Zapotecos, but his intentions having been frustrated by the heroic resistance of the Mixtecos, his caciques decided upon a direct invasion against the Zapotecos, and the Mexican armies took the road by Teotitlan, without touching the Mixteco possessions.

This measure was completely successful, as it allowed the Mexicans to penetrate into the territory of the Zapotecos and continue their route to Tehuantepec, with the view of extending their conquests towards the East. Whether it was from want of elements to repel the Mexican invasion or from strategic considerations, he opposed only a slight resistance. When the Mexicans were in possession of Tehuantepec, the Mixteco and Zapoteco kings formed an alliance, and uniting their forces, they charged upon the Mexicans, the first of these kings recovering his lost possessions. From the differences occurring between the two sovereigns during the expedition, there arose an enmity on the part of the Mixteco king who was desirous of domineering over his enemy's country, which he carried into effect by taking possession of various places and blocking up the population of Zachila. The king of the Zapotecos retired with his court to a small mountain called "the teat of Maria Sanchez." In this state both kings were found, when they were surprised by the Spanish invasion.

The Zapotecos as well as the Mixtecos were intelligent and industrious: they cultivated maize, fruit and cocoa, which besides game, served as their nutriment. The ruins which are met with in the neighbourhood of Teotitlan del Valle, prove the grandeur of these nations. Mitla or Lioba, (in the Zapoteco language, place of rest) was the sanctuary of their Gods, the palace of the high priest and the crypt of the kings, the building being divided into various compartments. It was there where the Zapotecos dissented from their culture by their barbarous and inhuman sacrifices, and where they displayed the greatest magnificence in the interment of their kings.

These palaces have always caused the admiration of travellers by the beautiful style of their decoration and construction, six monolith columns without either base or capitl being especially remarkable, so much so that Baron de Humboldt believed them to be the only ones in the New World. Sahagun says that among the ruins of the city of Tula, there might be seen at one time some columns in the figure of a sake that had the head for the base and the tail for the capital. In my last expedition to this town, guided by the most lively desire of investigating objects so useful towards acquiring a knowledge of historical facts, I discovered three blocks of a column, artistically sculptured, in which the correctness of style and good taste of the design were admirable : these blocks were made to be adjusted to each other in such a way that they would give the greatest solidity to the column when raised. These three masses measure : the first 0^m 63, the second 0^m 56 and the third 1^m 20 and the diameter of the three 0^m 83. Besides these masses and other curious objects, I found buried in an eminence that had been the seat of ancient Tollan, three monolith basaltic blocks of 2^m 60 in height by 1^m 0 in diameter. Among these blocks, perfectly well finished, some double columns are distinguished, with their oblique bases towards the front and their capitals terminating in two circles, intended for the volutes of an Ionic capital. Symmetrically placed in both blocks are seen four *tlapillis* or ornaments in the shape of a bow or knot, of which, it is likely that each one may represent the period of thirteen years and the four together the Tloltec age or century.

The Zapotecas, according to an article of the Mexican Dictionary of History and Geography, compose the greater part of the population of the Southern part of the Isthmus, and are without comparison, superior to the other Indians. The healthiness of the climate, the extraordinary fertility of the soil and the variety and richness of its productions, contribute towards the happiness of the inhabitants, who, since the most remote period of their history, have been distinguished for their progress in civilization. *

---

* Clavijero remarks that "they were civilized and industrious: that they had their laws, that they exercised the arts of the Mexicans, they had the same mode of computing time and the same paintings to perpetuate the recollection of events, in which were represented the creation of the world

Even in the days of the conquest, their acquaintance with mechanical arts was not at all scanty, and their well fortified towns did not fail to excite the admiration and awaken the jealousy of the old kings of Anahuac. Bernal Diaz on referring to the labors of the expedition to Tehuantepec in 1522, says: "When he saw the quantity of gold the inhabitants possessed, he ordered them to make him a pair of spurs of the best quality, giving them as a pattern one of his own, and indeed they proved very good."

The Indians of Tehuantepec display more than middling qualities and are intelligent, docile and vigorous : their appearance is remarkable for the symmetry of their forms, the singularity of their features and the energy and sprightliness of their character. The women are of a delicate figure, voluptuous and exceedingly lively: they are noted for the exquisite grace of their walk, their pleasing expression and their love for showy dresses; they are intriguing and of licentious customs, but are sober and laborious. Many of them manufacture textures of silk and cotton which are unequalled in Mexico. The inhabitatns of the town of Tehuantepec employ themselves in different occupations, and the shops of the carpenters, silversmiths, tanners, harnessmakers and bakers give a lively appearance to the place. The quantity of soap made there is very considerable and the exportation of prepared deer skins forms a very lucrative branch of trade.

The Indians of Juchitan, although less numerous than those of Tehuantepec, compose a very important part of the inhabitants of the Isthmus, for their superiority in everything to the others. They are daring, independent, industrious and sober, they have considerable strength and a high degree of capacity, and the usefulness of their services as journeymen in construction works or as laborers in the field, is not to be doubted. Their appearance is less agreeable than that of those of Tehuantepec, and their disposition not so docile ; a circumstance that may be attributed to their impatient character and their knowledge of the state of physical and mental degradation in which they find themselves.

the universal deluge and the confusion of tongues, although all mixed with fictions. The Zapotecos have been the most industrious of the people of New Spain, since the conquest: whilst there was a trade in silks, they cultivated the silk-worm, and it is to their labor that is owing all the cochineal imported into Europe, proceeding from Mexico from many years back up to the present time.

The number of these Indians who are extended over the central region of the territory of Oaxaca reaches 239,600 distributed in the following manner.

Principal Zapotecos . .	120,000	Valley of Oaxaca, Etla, Zumatlan Ejutla, Tlacolula and Ocotlan.
Nexitza Zapotecos. . .	40,000	Sierra of Villa Alta to the North East of Oaxaca.
Zapotecos Serranos of Ixtepeji	32,000	Sierra de Ixtlan, to the North East of Oaxaca.
Zapotecos Serranos of Cajones.	10,600	West of Oaxaca and South of Villa Alta.
Zapotecos Serranos of Miahuatlan	27.000	South of Ejutla and the capital.
Zapotecos of Tehuantepec	10,000	In the Isthmus.
	239,600	

The *Popolocos* occupy different districts, such as the South of the State of Puebla, the District of Acatlan, the North of Oaxaca, the District of Coixtlahuaca, where they are known by the name of *Chochos*, the East of Guerrero, the District of Tlapa, by the name of *Tlapanecos;* in Michoacan by that of *Tecos*, and in Guatemala by that of *Populacas* and formerly *Topes*.

Their number ascends to 34,700 individuals.

Señor Pimentel separates the *Popolacos* from the *Chuchones*, stating that both belong to the Mixteco-Zapoteco family.

The *Cuicatecos* appertain to the Mixtecos, are found at Cuicatlan to the North of Oaxaca, and consist of 10,000 individuals.

The *Chatinos*, a part of the Mixteca family, inhabit the region to the South of the capital, limited to the towns of Elotepec, Ixtayutla, Yola, Yuchatengo and the coast, and are composed of 8,000 individuals.

The *Papabucos*, a part of the Mixteca family, inhabit the town of Elotepec, and District of Zimatlan with 400 individuals.

The *Amusgos* are found in the South Eastern part of the State of Guerrero, in the District of Ometepec, on the confines of Oaxaca : they are also found in the latter State, bordering with the former in the parishes of San Pedro de los Amusgos, San Francisco Soyultepec and Cacahuaxtepec. Their number is 12,600.

The *Mazatecos* reside in the region to the North of Oaxaca, between the rivers Tonto and Quiotepec; they count 28,000.

The *Soltecos* are met with amongst the Chatinos, but in the last report from Oaxaca, the Solteco language does not appear as existing.

The *Chinantecos* are extended to the North of the Zapotecos and the Sierra of Villa Alta, to the number of 12,000.

According to Señor Pimentel work, the classification of these last is doubtful.

Summary of the Mixteco-Zapoteca family:

Mixtecos...	220,000
Zapotecos...	239,600
Popolocos...	34,700
Cuicatecos...	10,000
Chatinos...	8,000
Papabucos...	400
Amusgos...	12,600
Mazatecos...	28,000
Chinantecos...	12,000
Total...	565,300

XIV

THE MATLATZINCA OR PIRINDA FAMILY.

THE *Pirindas* or *Matlanzincas* who formerly inhabited the valley of Toluca and were the founders of that city, have almost completely disappeared, some few individuals only being met with as the remains of that nation in the town of Charo in the State of Michoacan. According to Señor Orozco y Berra and from the original data in my possession, for

which I am indebted to the three rectors of the Archbishop's palace of Mexico, it appears that there still exist *Matlanzincas*, speaking their own language in the the towns of San Martin and Santa Cruz, in the District of Temascaltepec of the Valley, in San Juan Azinco in the District of Ocuila; in San Mateo Mexicalzinco in that of Calimaya and in San Mateo of Temascaltepec.

The Matlatzincas "says Clavijero," formed a considerable state in the fertile valley of Toluca, and although the fame of their bravery might have been formerly great, they were, notwithstanding, subjected by King Axayactl, to the crown of Mexico.

According to Basalenque the Matlatzincas of Charo were originaries of Toluca and left their country in order to aid in a war against the people of Michoacan, locating themselves from Indaparapeo to Tiripitio, which was the centre of the kingdom, for which they were called *pirindas* or rather *pirintas*, which in the "tarasca" language signifies those of the middle.

Matlatzinco is a Mexican word which signifies place of nets "as it is composed of matlata" a net and the particle "tzinco" which means diminution.

The number of the Matlatzincos reaches 4,460 individuals.

XV

MAYA FAMILY.

This large family, whose number has decreased notably owing to the disastrous wars of casts, inhabits the peninsula of Yucatan, and extends itself with its divers languages over Tabasco, Chiapas and Guatemala and is also found in the Northern part of Veracruz, called the Huasteca, as appears by the classification of indigenous languages by Francisco Pimentel. In the peninsula of Yucatan they are found in two groups: that of the pacific Indians in the Southern regions, where they are incorporated with the other races in the towns and haciendas, and that of the insurrectionary Indians in the Eastern parts, the principal location of the latter being in Chan-Santa Cruz.

The *Punctunc* Indians are found in the vicinity of Palenque, in the State of Chiapas.

The *Lacandones* are in the Eastern portion of the same state, extending themselves to Guatemala and occupying themselves preferentially in hunting, fishing and the cultivation of maize and tobaco. They use bows and arrows which they manage with dexterity, their dress being composed of a shirt or jacket of "manta" (cotton domestics) which reaches half way to the knee, and of a band of raw silk, dyed a red color. Obliged to traverse through the woods, they use no hat, and are frequently found to be bald from the loss of their long hair,-torn away little by little, by the dense brambles and briers in the bushy places into which they penetrate. The women wear folded skirts and *huipilli*.

The Lacandones smoke tobacco and are not fond of fermented liquors. They trade in tobacco, vegetable wax, honey and the skins of the animals they hunt, receiving in exchange glass beads, hatchets and salt which the natives of Chiapas take them; they live in clans without knowing any form of government or system of religion, and only by their gestures is it supposed that they tribute adoration to the Sun.

The *Petenes* or *Peten-itzaes* in the Southern part of Yucatan, inhabit the neighbourhood of the lake Peten-Ixta.

The *Chañabales*, *Comitecos* and *Jocolobales* are extended over Zapaluta, Comitan and Chicomucelo in Chiapas.

The *Choles* or *Mopanes* form a tribe that has been established since a very remote period in the Eastern part of Chiapas and in Verapaz in Guatemala.

The *Chortis* or *Chortes* are found on the borders of Montagina in Guatemala.

The *Cakchis*, *Caichis*, *Cachis* or *Cakgis*, in Guatemala.

The *Ixilis* or *Izilis* in the same Republic.

The *Coxoh* in the same Republic.

The *Quiches* or *Utlatecos* in Chiapas and Guatemala. The former kingdom of Quiché was the most powerful and civilized of Guatemala, as is testified by the ruins of a city of the first order, Utlatan, which rivalled with the palaces of Moctezuma and the Incas. Their capital was Ralimamet or Tecpancuauhtemalan. They understood hieroglyphic inscriptions and accustomed human sacrifices.

The *Zutuchil*, *Zutugil*, *Atitecas* and *Zacapulas* inhabited Guatemala.

The *Cachiqueles* or Cachiquiles, also in Guatemala.

The *Tzotziles*, *Zotziles*, *Tzinantecos* or *Cinantecos* dwelt in the Northern, Central and Southern districts of Chiapas. The city of Tzinacantlan (habitation of bats) was the capital of the *Quelenes* and afterwards of the *Tzotziles*, whose descendants and especially those of the town of Chamula are strong, of a domineering character and ably disposed to the arts, whereby they exercise several trades advantageously: they are gardeners, tanners, shoemakers, lime-burners, stone-masons, carpenters and manufacturers of harps, violins and guitars, all instruments highly appreciated for their superior construction (Plate 8, group 1st).

The *Tzendales* or *Zendales* exist in many parts of Chiapas (Plate 8, group 1st.)

The *Mames* or *Memes*, *Zaklohpakap* are found in Tapachula, in Chiapas and in Guatemala. The *Mames* composed a powerful State in Guatemala, that extended over Quetzaltenango, Huehuetenango and Soconusco in Chiapas and at other places in Guatemala and San Salvador. The ancient Mames of Soconusco governed independently until the moment of their being conquered by the Olmecas, who, without doubt, were of that nation to which Ixtilzochitl attributed the construction of the pyramid of Cholula, previous to the Toltecas. To free themselves from the yoke of the Olmecas the Mames immigrated to other parts, removing as far as Nicaragua: those who remained at Soconusco, suffered another invasion from the Toltecas, who conquered them, an event; which doubtless ocurred at the period of the destruction and dispersion of that people. The Toltecas, united to the Mames, sustained various wars with their neighbours the Kiclies, until being defeated by the king Kikab II, they found themselves obliged to hide in the woods.

Later on, Ahuixotl, the 18th king of Mexico, carried his conquests as far as Guatemala; Soconusco from that date remaining subject to the Mexican Empire.

The *Atchis* or *Atches* inhabited Guatemala.

The *Huastecos* with their dialects, in the region comprising the Northern part of Veracruz and the South East of San Luis, limited by the Gulf coasts from the bar of Tuxpan to that of Tampico. The origin of the Huastecos, like that of the other indigenous races is doubtful. On the arrival of the Spaniards they inhabited, independently of the kingdom of Texcoco and the empire of Mexico, the places situated on the frontiers of these two nations. *Huaxtlan* signifies a place where *huaxi* abounds, a fruit known by the name of *huaje*.

The *Haitianos*, *Quizquejas* or *Itis* with their affinities the *Cubanos*, *Boriquas* and *Jamaicas* were residents of the Antilles.

According to the chronicler Herrera, the former inhabitants of Yucatan related that their ancestors had come from the East, and others relying with more or less certainty on the classification of languages and in the identity of ancient monuments revealed by various ruins, imagine to have discovered an immigration from the West and the traces of this peregrination in the ruins of Comalcalco in Tabasco. In the peninsula of Yucatan, these pyramids are again observed, with the small hillocks called *cues*, with the singular circumstance of their being hollow, in like manner to what is noticed in the pyramid of the Moon at Teohotihuacan, it being also remarked that in the *cue* at Yucatan, explored by Mr. Stephens, the interior compartments were distinct.

The Mayas having united under the command of a monarch, formed a vast empire, whose capital was the city of Mayapan, and which was afterwards divided into various States governed by special rulers. The Aztecs designated the positions occupied by the Mayas and the natives of Tabasco by the name of *Onohualcos*, which means "independent provinces."

Torquemada states that the Mayas inhabited the kingdom of Yucatan, which covered an extent of more than three hundred leagues, and that it was well populated and administered by individual authorities. They were ruled by good laws and customs; they enjoyed peace and justice, which is an argument that favors their good government, and he attributes this particularly to their all speaking the same language, and is not a little surprised that so many people and so extended over a place of so many leagues, should understand with each other in the same dialect.

Yucatan was discovered by Francisco Fernandez de Cordova in 1517 and was conquered by Captain Francisco de Montejo in 1527. The multitude of stone buildings and temples which the Spaniards met with and the celebrated ruins of palaces which have caused the admiration of intelligent travellers, demonstrate the highly advanced state of civilization of a people whose origin is entirely unknown.

The Mayas understood hieroglyphic inscriptions and computed time in in the same way as the Mexicans. Their descendants have now forgotten this knowledge and limit themselves to regulate time by the movement of the stars. Agriculture is their principal calling and they dedicate themselves particularly to growing maize, subjecting themselves to the system of their ancestors. They are also engaged in the manufacture of sacks, hammocks and cordage of henequen and in making straw hats. Their ordinary food consists of boiled vegetables seasoned with salt, "chile" or pepper, and sometimes with orange or lemon juice. At their feasts they have an abundance of game, which they roast underground, after being previously heated according to the method generally adopted throughout the country. This dish is known by the name of *barbacoa*. They frequently intoxicate themselves with "aguardiente" and "pitarilla," which is a drink made from an infusion of the peel of a plant called *balché*, sweetened with honey.

Timid, crafty and mistrustful they attack their enemies with superior numbers, and after a defeat scatter themselves in the depths of the thickets to meet again at some place previously designated. They are good marksmen and manage the "machete" (a species of cutlass) with dexterity. A hut built of sticks covered with mud, with its roof made of guano or turf, some common hammocks and a few utensils of absolute necessity for domestic use, is all that is required by a family of the Maya Indians. Music, which preserves its traditional rhythm and of which a sample is given at the end of this work, and dancing, form the constant manifestation of their rejoicings. They accompany their characteristic sonnets with the harsh tones of a small flute, with those of a turtle's shell beaten by a deer's horn and by those of a "*mitote*" a wooden instrument of cylindrical shape and hollow, of about one yard in length and one third in diameter, diminished and completely open at its foot and perforated in the upper part, forming two small languets or plates that vibrate on being struck by two small wooden balls, producing a confused sound. This instrument under the name of *teponaxtle* is very general among the Mexican natives.

Like to all the Indian races of Mexico, the Mayas are idolaters, preferring to devote their principal acts of worship to images of the Saints than to the Supreme Being. They are under the impression that the souls of those who die return to this world, and in order that they should not lose their way, they mark the road from the burial place to their home, with lime.

Their belief in witches and ghosts increases their errors: they fear *Balám*, the Lord of the fields, to such a degree that they do not commence their agricultural labors, before first venerating this ideal being with incense. At times this spectre is a woman who, in the costume of the "mestizas" and wearing in her hair the fruit of a plant called *sachextabay*, flies away or approaches, hastens or retards her steps, disappears or allows herself to be reached, if the one who follows her is a lover; who at last loses his senses, his fascination arriving to such a degree that he is seized with fever on finding his illusion destroyed and on embracing within his arms a figure full of thorns, with the feet as thin as those of a fowl, in place of the enchanting "mestiza." At other times it is a giant who haunts the towns at midnight and places his feet on each of the side walks to prevent any one from passing, and if any careless passenger should take the middle path, he closes his legs and crushes him. Lastly other phantoms continually disturb them and terrify them with noises.

The dress of the Maya Indians consists of a white cotton shirt falling outside of the drawers which are wide and reach down to the knee, a handkerchief, a straw hat and sandals with leathern soles, tied with henequen strings. When they are at work in the field they undress themselves and only wear a "pampanilla" or covering to screen their nakedness, which they call *huit*, made of a piece of cotton cloth around the waist, the ends of which pass between the thighs and are again tied at the waist.

The Indian women, inside their houses, only use fustian or a white cotton skirt, reaching from the waist to the knee; their personal cleanliness is remarkable, as they consider it irrational not to bathe themselves every day. When they visit the towns they cover their heads with a white cotton garment or perhaps with a red handkerchief, whose ends fall over the shoulders, and change their dress to a "huipilli" and fustian embroidered white colored thread.

The Indian women are generally sober, economical, hospitable and well disposed to work for the purpose of helping their husbands, but on the other hand are very vindictive; so much so that they never forget an offense as long as they remain without avenging it. Their domestic labors are reduced to grinding maize, making *tortillas* (pancakes), *atole* (gruel) and *pozole*, washing, sowing and spinning and weaving ordinary cotton stuffs.

The Indians of Yucatan are robust and of a little more than medium stature, they are round-faced, their hair is black, straight and thick and they have little or no beard. Their forehead is low, the eyes bright and expressive, the cheek bones projecting, the mouth regular, the lips thin and with splendid teeth: the neck is thick and the breast and shoulders broad; the arms, thighs and legs strong and muscular; the color of their skin is copperish and becomes darker by constant exposure to the sun; in the women it is much clearer. Among the latter there are many of a pretty appearance, well formed and with a graceful walk and a sweet voice;

but the rude and habitual labors to which they dedicate themselves from childhood, soon cause their attractiveness to fade.

These are some of the most characteristic traits of the Indians of Yucatan, who by their uninterrupted insurrections have devastated their beautiful and opulent country.

The reports that I have consulted and very particularly those that were furnished me by D. Santiago Mendez, who was the Governor of Yucatan, have allowed me to give these statements regarding the race referred to.

In the numerical part, I shall limit myself solely to the people of this family that belong to the Mexican Republic.

Maya Indians of Yucatan,

Comprising Chiapas and Tabasco . . .	268,000
Chañabales	6,500
Choles	4,000
Quichés	3,000
Tzotziles	36,000
Tzeendales	34,000
Mames	3,000
Huaxtecos	37,000
Maya family	391,500

XVI

CHONTAL FAMILY.

THE *Chontal* Indians inhabit the State of Tabasco principally, and in a scarce number Guerrero, Oaxaca, Guatemala and Nicaragua. Formerly they were distinguished by their ferocity, but their character being modified with the process of time, they have lost their barbarous instincts, although they have advanced but little in the road of civilization. They are brave, of a robust constitution and in general indolent, and are satisfied by laboring to obtain a little maize, cocoa, tobacco and aguardiente to fill their requirements. Their religious ceremonies and particularly those of the festivities of the Santa Cruz, serve rather as a pretext for dissoluteness than as a commemoration of the services celebrated by the Catholic church. On these occasions the women prepare the *chorote* and the men collect bees-wax and honey and kill an ox or a lizard on the day they make their candles. They commence the festivity by all proceeding to the church, carrying the offerings they are about to render the Saint of their devotion, these consisting in large baskets filled with parboiled trout and rations of meat, and in 25 or 30 jars of *chorote* or *posole*, a beverage made of ground maize, prepared and boiled in water. On presenting the offering, they pray to the Saint to restore health to those who are sick ; to fatten some domestic animal; to deliver them from the bites of snakes and from all other evils, or again to multiply their crops. They offer the provisions to the Saint, in order that he may eat of the substance, whilst it is they who finish by profiting thereby and drinking to satiety the *balché*, a fermented beverage made from the juice of the sugar-cane, burnt corn and molasses, and winding up by dancing their favorite pantomimic dances in the church itself, such as the *caballito* (little horse) the *pelicano* (the pelican) the *gigante* (the giant) and Saint Michael, dressed in the old Spanish fashion, with blue stockings, shoes with cascabels, knee-breeches with motley-colored fringes and a handkerchief tied round the neck ; this grotesque figure being completed by the hideous wooden masks that covered the face.

The *Chontals* are fanatic and superstitious to the degree of attributing their infirmities to witchcraft; and apply the remedies that are prescribed to them by their quack doctors who are practically acquainted with the properties and virtues of certain herbs and roots : they also believe in the transmigration of souls into the bodies of animals.

The Indians were domineered by the Spaniards more by the force of persuasion than by that of arms.
To day, they may be numbered in all at 30,000 individuals. See the *Chontal* types in Plate 8, group 2$^{nd.}$

XVII

LANGUAGES ORIGINATING FROM NICARAGUA.

The *Huaves*, called by some *Huazontecos*, according to Pimentel, proceed from Nicaragua and occupy the narrow strips of land that are left free by the large lakes *("albuferas")* to the South of the Isthmus of Tehuantepec, and inhabit the places called Santa Maria del Mar, San Mateo del Mar, San Francisco del Mar, San Dionisio del Mar and Ixhuatan; their number ascends to 3,000 individuals who live divided into four factions and in the most complete anarchy as regards local interests.

The strifes they maintained between themselves or against their neighbours, decided them to emigrate from their native country, to launch upon the sea in frail barks and to navigate along the coasts in the direction of Tehuantepec, of whose plains they took possession and extended themselves to the foot of the cordillera, but not without overcoming the Mixes who were the owners of the land and obliging them to seek refuge in the depths of the mountainous ranges. The *Huave* settlers being first conquered by the hosts of Moctezuma and afterwards reduced by the Mixtecos and Zapotecos united, circumscribed their lands to the narrowest limits.

In the work entitled "Reconnoisance of Tehuantepec, 1844," the following notices appear:

"The *Huaves* differ in their appearance from the other inhabitants of the State of Oaxaca, being generally robust and well formed. They habitually go very nearly naked and their occupations are reduced to the fishery in which they do a considerable trade. The *Chiapanecos* also natives of Nicaragua, as results from the comparison of their language with others of that Republic, have so mixed themselves with the so-called *Ladinos* of Chiapas that they have caused their habits, their customs and their dialect to disappear."

Clavijero expresses himself in the following terms regarding this tribe:

The *Chiapanecos*, if we are to give credit to their traditions, were the first populators of the New World. They said that Votan, the grandson of that venerable old man who built the great bark to save himself and his family from the Deluge, and one of those who undertook the work of the grand edifice which was made to reach to heaven, went by express command of the Lord to populate that land. They said, also, that the first populators had come from Northern parts and when they arrived at Soconusco, they separated, some going to inhabit the country of Nicaragua and others remaining in Chiapas.

This nation, as related by some historians, was not governed by a King, but by two military chiefs, who were nominated by the priests. They thus maintained themselves, until the last Mexican kings made them submit to their crown. They made the same use of their paintings as the Mexicans, and had the same mode of computing time, but adopted different figures from them to represent the years, months and days.

XVIII

THE APACHE FAMILY.

The *Apaches* with the divers names of their several tribes, *Chiricahues, Tontos, Mimbreños, Gileños, Mescaleros, Sacramenteños, Carrizaleños, Mogollones, Lipanes, Faraones, Navajoes* and others, live a wandering life in that part of the United States bordering upon our frontiers. They make their incursions into Sonora, by the District of Altar and Magdalena, as those denominated *Gileños* and *Mescaleros* effect the same by the North East, invading the whole of the State. The Apaches of Chihuahua are spread over the neighbourhood of Janos and like those of Sonora, employ themselves by preference in stealing cattle, and in assassinating and rejoicing in the martyrdom of their victims.

These savages are exceedingly fleet, both in traversing the vast plains and in climbing the rugged eminences of the mountains, and are moreover excellent horsemen. Their arms are the bow and arrow, and a lance with a flint point; they use a leather quiver and a shield or *chimal* of leopard's skin, ornamented with feathers, and with small mirrors in the centre, with which they succeed in dazzling the enemy.

Endowed with a belligerent character and of ferocious instincts, they are nearly always at war with the whites, with the *Comanches* and even among themselves. Their mode of warfare consists in surprises to ensure the triumph and in retreats to evade a combat with a superior enemy, but without failing to prove themselves brave and resolute when the occasion to fight presents itself. They fly with extreme velocity and endeavour to allure their persecutors to a convenient spot in order to fall upon them unexpectedly, and celebrate their victories by infernal dances around the scalps torn from their victims. They make use of smoke for their telegraphic signals whether it be for congregating together, for communicating some danger or for carrying out some expedition.

They believe in a Supreme Being, and without rendering him external homage, they venerate him under the name of *Yaxtaxitaxitanne*, which signifies Captain of Heaven, and in order to assuage the anger of the bad Spirit, they have their prophets and soothsayers who are highly esteemed among them. So great is their horror of epidemic infirmities that they fly to very distant places and do not return to their former abodes until after they have assured themselves of the disappearance of the pest. They go nearly naked and are so uncleanly that it is generally believed that the wild animals foreknow by their scent the approximation of these savages. The Apache women do not comb themselves during the time their fathers or their husbands are in campaign.

The Indians belonging to the Atapasca nation, were instructed in the Christian faith by Franciscan priests, shortly after the conquest. They are not known to have any system of government, as they only obey the orders of the chiefs of the tribes, who are selected from amongst the most able and courageous in the time of war. These Indians, in their language, apply the name of Apaches to those who rebel, therefore it is to their insurrections that they owe their own name.

They are much addicted to hunting deer, wild boars, "cibolos" or Mexican bulls, black bears and wild goats and rams. Their dress consists of a strip of linen, passing between their thighs and fastened at the waist, and in leggings of deer-skin with fringes ornamented with beads and garnished with leather strings; their shoes called "*teguas*" of the same skin are joined to the leggings. They pierce their ears and wear ear-rings and pendants of metal, and in their hair they fasten a long false braid adorned with trinkets, shells or silver buckles.

(The women who are as active as the men in their habits, use very short garments of deer skin or kid, which they call *tlacalce*, with fringes of leather strings on whose edges are hung cascabels, tassels and red beads ; they also wear a kind of jacket called *bietli*, made of an entire deerskin, open in front, ornamented exactly the same as the rest of their dress, and they also use "*teguas*."

The Apaches are strong, of a bronze color, with long hair and without any beard. They have all the faculties of the senses admirably developed, of which circumstance they avail themselves in their depredations. They marry with all the women they choose and dissolve the matrimony when they please, sometimes returning their consort to the father, brother or relation, if she has been the cause of the separation, and at others paying back the price of the marriage contract, or in case of infidelity they punish her by cutting off her nose.

The barbarous customs of the Apaches are specially exhibited in cases of death. If an Indian dies, the men cut off their long hair and make incisions in their faces, arms and legs with sharp-edged flints, or wound themselves in the breast on the side of the heart, and the women burn their clothes and throw themselves naked upon prickly plants.

Horse-flesh is the favorite food of the Apaches, giving the preference afterwards to the other quadrupeds chased both by the men and the women. They also feed themselves with wild fruit, maize, beans and pumpkins which the women cultivate on a very limited scale. They have no other enjoyment than that of drinking the liquor distilled from the "maguey" and that of smoking tobacco.

The Apaches, by their mistrustful character, prefer living in the asperities of the mountainous regions, where they build their circular hovels with branches of trees and skins of quadrupeds, and are continually changing their domicile, according to the season or their incursionary plans.

The *Mescaleros* inhabit the watering places and mountain ranges near to Coyame and San Carlos, formerly military posts :

The *Lipanes* to the East of San Carlos and banks of the river Bravo, by Santa Rosa :

The *Gileños* on the banks of the river Gila :

The *Sacramenteños*, in the Sierra of Sacramento :

The *Carrizaleños* and *Coyoteros* in the Sierra de Arados, Carmen and Fierro, in the vicinity of Carrizal:

The *Mimbreños* in the Sierra de los Mimbres:

The *Faraones* in the Sierras between the River Grande and the river Pecos:

The *Xicarillas* are a branch of the Faraones:

The *Navajoes* in various "rancherias" of the Sierra de Navajo, and are those who are the most towards the North.

For the special reasons that I have already indicated, the number of Apaches that inhabit the States of Sonora, Chihuahua, and Coahuila, within our territory, cannot be stated correctly, but by the data that I have been enabled to consult, they may be calculated at 10,000

XIX

THE OTHOMI OR HIU-HIU FAMILY.

The *Othomies* including all the indigenous Indians who speak the languages of this family, occupy a large extent of the territory of the Republic.

The principal *Othomies* are met with in the States of Guanajuato and Queretaro, and the Western part of Hidalgo, and in a part of the North Western region of Mexico. Isolated from this principal group, they are also found in the town of Ixtengo, pertaining to Tlaxcala, in a part of the Sierra of Zacualtipan in the State of Hidalgo, and in some places situated to the South of Zacatlan in the State of Puebla, in some of the towns in the district of Tuxpan, mixed with the Mexicans; in the parish of Zitacuaro in the State of Michoacan, in union with the Mazahuas, and in the town of Santa Maria del Rio in San Luis Potosi.

The *Serranos* in the Sierra-gorda of Guanajuato:.

The *Mazahuas* inhabit a great part of the Districts of Ixtlahuaca and the Villa del Valle in the State of Mexico, and in the parishes of Taximaroa, Tlalpujahua and Zitacuaro in Michoacan.

The *Pames* are established in the ancient mission of Cerro-prieto (in the parish of Jacala, State of Hidalgo); in the town of Santa Maria Acapulco in Queretaro, and in the mission of the Purisima Concepcion, at Arnedo, about a league from Xichu in the State of Guanajuato. The principal body of the Pames is found in the Eastern provinces of San Luis Potosi:

The *Jonaces* or Mecos, so called by the Spanish missionaries, inhabited a part of the Sierra-gorda of Guanajuato.

According to certain writers, the *Othomies* constitute the most ancient population of Anahuac. Expelled by the Toltecas from the places where the latter founded or rebuilt Tula, according to Clavijero, they extended their province to the Northern part of the Valley of Mexico, at 90 miles from the capital. Many persons have imagined to have discovered an analogy between the Chinese language and the Othomi, one of these being our distinguished philologer Father Najera, but this idea has been lately combatted by Pimentel in his classification of languages. For many centuries, these Indians remained in a savage state, preserving very vague recollections of their peregrinations, wandering among the mountains and subsisting principally by hunting game, until being subjected to the kings of Texcoco in the 15th century, they began to live in society, although many of them continued in their primitive condition. Up to the present, their descendants have improved but little upon these uncultured people.

Mistrust, indifference and ignorance are revealed in the spirit of their character, which among the Indians of the Sierra, is shown to be astute, hypocritical and treacherous, differing in this peculiar respect from the other natives, who without being free from other defects, possess in exchange very good qualities.

The Othomies are composed of 450,000 individuals, including the Serranos and Jonaces.

The *Mazahuas*, who in the time of the Aztec empire pertained to the kingdom of Tlacopan, and whose dominions were bordered by Michoacan, consist of some 50,000.

On the missionary Father Soriano treating of the character, habits and customs of the Pames, he expresses himself in the following manner: "The nature of these Indians and of all those in America is indefinible, as the more one treats with them, the less one knows them: to deal with them is a slow and protracted martyrdom; in general it is rare that they requite a benefit, as if one gives them anything, they say, it is not given me for nothing. They are as malicious as they are ignorant. The men are generally very indolent and are only fond of roving through the mountains like wild beasts. It was for this that they so much disliked our doctrine, in the principles to which the ministers subjected them, even so far as to mutiny and attempt the lives of the missionaries. The men are ingenious and humble: with good treatment they will learn anything; the women are very cleanly, useful and industrious; they make good cotton cloth (manta), *hucpiles* (petticoats), mats and very curious trunks. The woman carries the water, brings the fire-wood and in fact does the most of the labor, whilst the husband is accustomed to lie down to sleep. The houses of the Pames are of grass, turf or of palm-leaves; they walk bare-footed; their dress approaches to nakedness, as the most of them use a covering for the head or a blanket: their food consists of toasted maize and many herbs. The majority are still inclined to idolatry; they yet retain many abuses and nearly all of them believe in soothsayers and witches. Formerly these Pames venerated Moctezuma greatly, to whose dominion they were subjected for many years, and whom they looked upon as a deity; they all worshipped the Sun for their God. Others had their particular deities such as idols of stone or of wood. They also have their dances, calling the houses where they hold them, *catiz manchi*, which means to say "virgin house." They give these dances at sowing-time, when the grain is in the ear, and on gathering in the maize, to the sound of a tabor and many fifes, and very leisurely commence to play their doleful and melancholy tunes. The soothsayer sits in the middle with his small drum and with many gestures stares at the company; he then rises slowly and after dancing many dances he sits down on a bench and pricks the calf of his leg with a thorn and sprinkles the blood over the corn-field by way of a blessing, and before this ceremony, no one dared to take a single cob, but left the crop intact: after the ceremony, they paid the soothsayer *(cajoo* or *hechicero)* and all comenced to eat corn-cobs, and afterwards gave themselves up to intoxication, to which the Indians are much addicted. . . The faith that most of these Indians have in these soothsayers, is very great; the latter have their superiors who are called *Maidajaboo*, which signifies "great soothsayer," and this *canaille* is employed in curing the sick, which is done by breathing all over their bodies, and then preserving the breath in a small earthen jar, perfectly well covered up and afterwards buried near the idols or stones to which I have referred . . . . These accursed rabble called *cojoos* or wizards, are venerated by them, and looked upon in the same way that the Catholics look upon their priests. . . . When a woman gives birth to a child, and after she is able to walk, they fix upon her feast day, and afterwards they take her out of the house giving many turns, and if the child is a girl they bring her a pitcher called *oaxaquita* and other articles, and finish by all getting drunk. When any one dies in a house they open a door for the body to go out of, and if the body is carried through the one already made, they close this and open another."

Of all the indigenous tribes referred to, the Othomies, and more especially the inhabitants of the Sierras or mountainous regions, are remarkable for their extremely mistrustful character and their bad inclinations, contrasting essentially in this respect with the former Mexican race.

In Plate 8, group 3rd, the types of the principal Othomies and those of the Pames are represented.

The total number of the latter may be calculated at 25,000.

Total number of the Othomi family:

    Principal Othomies. . . 550,000
    Mazahuas 50,000
    Pames. 25,000
                Total. . 625,000

RECAPITULATION.

THE population of the Mexican United States reaches the number of 9.495,157 inhabitants, in which number are comprised 3.517,580 native Indians distributed in the following manner, excluding those families who do not inhabit the Mexican territory:

MEXICAN family extending over the States of Sinaloa, Jalisco, Aguascalientes, Durango, South of San Luis Potosi, Colima, the coasts of Michoacan, Guerrero, Morelos, Mexico, Puebla, the Federal District, Hidalgo, Tlaxcala, Veracruz and in less number, in Tabasco, Oaxaca and Chiapas	1.503,270
SONORA or Opata-Pima family, which pertains to the States of Sonora, Sinaloa, Durango, Chihuahua, Jalisco and Zacatecas	69,150
GUAICURA and Cochimi-Laimon family in Lower California	2,500
Carried forward .	1.574,920

Brought forward. 1.574,920

SERI family, on the coasts of Sonora and the Island of Tiburon. 200

TARASCA family, in the State of Michoacan, part of Guanajuato, in the Valley of Mazamitla in Jalisco, and in some few parts of Guerrero, bordering on Michoacan. 200,000

ZOQUE-MIXE family, in the Western region of Chiapas, to the North of the Sierra Madre, in a small part of the South of Tabasco, and in mountainous districts of the Isthmus of Tehuantepec. 47,600

TOTONACA family, to the North of the State of Puebla, in the Sierra of Huachinango, and in the State of Vera Cruz, in the zone comprised between the rivers Chachalacas and Cazones, bounded by the Huasteca 85,000

MIXTECO-ZAPOTECA family, in the greater part of the State of Oaxaca, the District of Acatlan in Puebla and the Eastern portion of Guerrero. 565,300

MATLATZINCA OR PIRINDA family, in the town of Charo, State of Michoacan and in those of San Martin and Santa Cruz, in the District of Temascaltepec, in San Juan Azinco, in the environs of Ocuila, in San Mateo Mexicalcinco, in that of Calimaya and in San Mateo in the mineral district of Temascaltepec, all in the State of Mexico. 4,460

MAYA family in Yucatan and Campeachy, Tabasco, Chiapas and in the Huasteca, between the States of Tamaulipas, San Luis Potosi and Veracruz 391,500

CHONTAL family in the States of Tabasco, Oaxaca and Guerrero. 30,600

HUAVE family, originating from Nicaragua, on the Southern coast of Tehuantepec and in the central part of Chiapas 3,000

APACHE family in Sonora and Chihuahua . . . 10,000

Carried forward 2.912,580

Brought forward. 2.912,580
OTHOMI family in the States of Mexico, Michoacan, Hidalgo, Queretaro, Guanajuato, the Eastern portion of San Luis Potosi and other parts isolated from the principal group. 625,000

3.537,580

Not without great difficulty have I been enable to acquire the greatest possible amount of data which permit me to estimate and classify the population of the Republic in the following manner:

20 per Cent of the European race and nearest
descendants of the Spaniards. 1.899,031
43 per Cent of the mixed race 4.082,918
37 per Cent of the native Indian race . . 3.513,208

9.495,157

In 1810 according to the census of Don Fernando Navarro y Noriega, as appears in the "Political Essay of New Spain," the population of this part of the American continent, consisted of 6,122,354 inhabitants classified as follows:

Europeans and American Spaniards. . . . 1.097,928
Indians 3.676,281
Mixed races or casts 1.338,706
Secular ecclesiastics 4.229
Regular ecclesiastics 3,112
Nuns. 2,098

6.122,354

These statistical data suggested the most important considerations. Baron Humboldt remarked in his Political Essay, as a consolatory idea for humanity, that the increase of the Indian race was a fact and that the extensive region that was comprehended under the general name of New Spain, was found to be more populated than before the arrival of the Spaniards. The statement of this distinguished traveller, assuring this fact might have found its confirmation in the events that were occurring at the period to which his work referred; but as it was then impossible to foresee the numerous causes that might be brought to bear against so respectable an opinion, that circumstance, then so propitious to the Indian race, has since taken another aspect.

The indolence of the Indians, their attachment to their ancient customs, their bad nourishment, their little shelter against the inclemency of the weather, their wretched attendance in their sicknesses, and other adverse causes which I have pointed out in the course of this work, have contributed towards the degeneration and decline of the race.

On comparing the census of 1810 with that of 1875, in the part relating to the indigenous race, the decrease may be observed. As an evidence that the cipher of the last census is not too high, as some seem to pretend, it will suffice to fix attention on the fact that the mixed race is that which prevails in the greater part of the Republic and that the number of the Indian race has diminished remarkably in the Northern domains, even to such a degree, in some of the States, as to be reduced to a nullity. Thus it is, that any error that may have been committed in the calculations, notwithstanding the care and prudence with which I have been guided in forming them, would alter that cipher in but very little, and would not influence in the least against this general conclusion: that *the Indian race has decreased and continues on the road of its decline*, unless civilization and other unforeseen causes should modify these lamentable results, converting them into others of a more favorable character.

That manifest destiny is successively observed from North to South. In the States of Tamaulipas, New Leon and Coahuila and in the major extent of San Luis Potosi, Zacatecas and Aguascalientes, there now remains nothing more than the reminiscence of their ancient and warlike inhabitants: in Chihuahua the mixed race has taken the lead by exiling the Tarahumares to the mountain wilds and the Apaches to the deserts of Janos: Sonora, in spite of the importance of some tribes, loses much of its Indian population: Durango scarcely retains the rests of the Tepehuanes: in Sinaloa and Jalisco, the Indian element is gradually disappearing and to conclude, Michoacan itself, once ruled by the indomitable Tarascos, has entered upon its decline. Only in the Southern States, that so far have not exhibited the effects of that law of desting, to which it would seem the Indian race is condemned, is a greater density of population to be found.

The decay of this race becomes still more palpable on comparing their number with that of the other two, which have attained a natural increase, but in order that the comparison should be more exact, it is requisite to deduct from the census of 1810, the numbers that were represented by the populations of the former provinces of New Mexico, Texas and Upper California, which no longer belong to the Mexican territory.

The census of 1810 becomes reduced in the following form:

Europeans and American Spaniards including the ecclesiastics	1.106,041
Indians	3.646,032
Casts	1.311,943
	6.064,016
Census of 1875	9.495,157
Increase of the population in 65 years.	3.431,141

From the preceding data it appears that the European race nearly doubled its population in the space of 65 years, and at the rate of 1,1 per Cent of increase per year; that the mixed race has trebled it at the rate of 3,25; and that the native race by its incorporation with the preceding and for the other causes indicated in the course of this work, has diminished at the rate of 0, 058 per Cent per annum.

If other germs of destruction did not exist in the Indian race and only its incorporation with the mixed race should have acted against its augmentation, that lamentable decrease in the mass of its population would not be observed, against which many favorable circumstances ought to have an influence, such as the strong constitutions of their individuals, their resistance to the inclemencies of the weather, their naturalization to every climate and the early proclivity of the females to pregnancy and their extraordinary fecundity.

Considering all these circumstances, the natural increase of the Indian race ought, at the least, to have doubled its number, and have reached up to the present time 7 millones.

I now conclude this work by stating that the white race has had a natural increment: that in the mixed race the increase is greater, owing to the incorporation of the Indian race and that as regards the latter no indications whatever are to be observed that might tend to repress their declension.

CARTA ETNOGR[

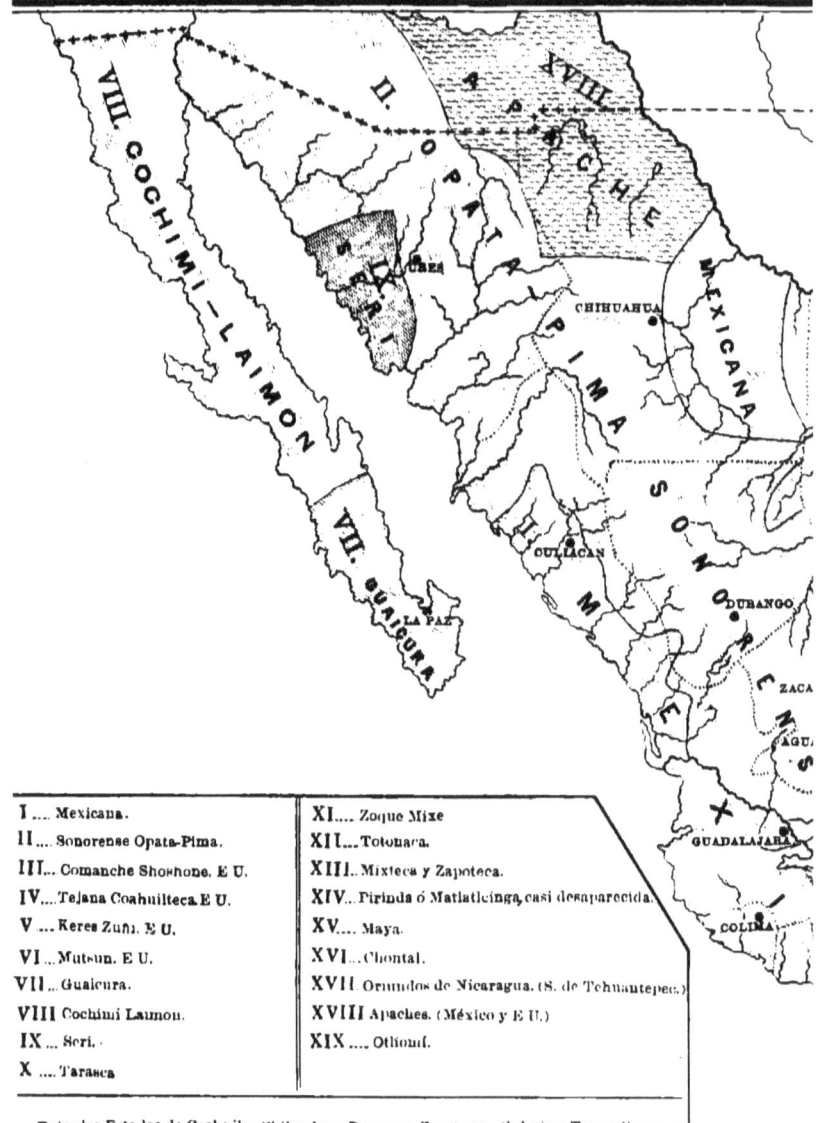

I.... Mexicana.
II.... Sonorense Opata-Pima.
III.... Comanche Shoshone. E U.
IV.... Tejana Coahuilteca. E U.
V ... Keres Zuñi. E U.
VI ... Mutsun. E U.
VII ... Guaicura.
VIII Cochimi Laimon.
IX ... Seri.
X .... Tarasca

XI.... Zoque Mixe
XII.... Totonaca.
XIII.. Mixteca y Zapoteca.
XIV.. Pirinda ó Matlatlcinga, casi desaparecida.
XV.... Maya.
XVI... Chontal.
XVII. Orundos de Nicaragua. (S. de Tehuantepec.)
XVIII Apaches. (México y E U.)
XIX .... Othomí.

Entre los Estados de Coahuila, Chihuahua, Durango, Zacatecas, S. Luis y Tamaulipas, se encuentra la region antes habitada por las siguientes tribus: 1. Los Tobosos, tribu Apache; 2. Los Irritilas; 3. Los Cuachiles, de los cuales, segun se cree, descienden los Huicholes, de la Familia Opata-Pima; 4. Los Tamaulipecos.

CA DE MÉXICO.

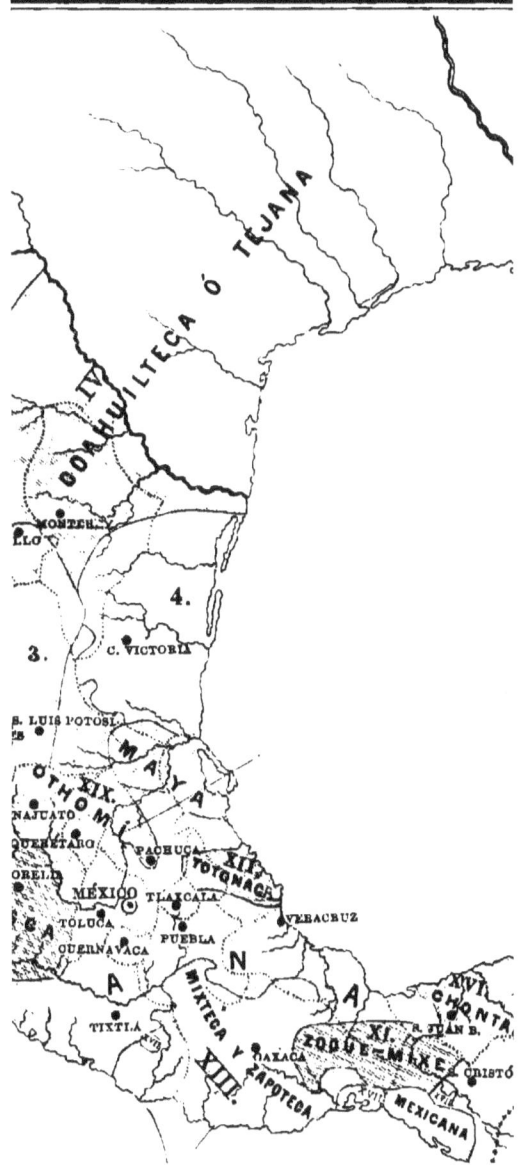

N.º 4
EL CAFÉ.

www.ingramcontent.com/pod-product-compliance
Lightning Source LLC
Chambersburg PA
CBHW030300170426
43202CB00009B/816